CUT OFF YOUR CREDIT

visual poetry by Russell Evans

For Wendy
and
Alfie, Zoe, Esme, Tom and Margot

This book is a work of original poetic art.

First paperback edition June 2025

ISBN 978-1-960991-49-2 (paperback)

Published by Raw Earth Ink
PO Box 39332
Ninilchik, AK 99639
www.raw-earth-ink.com

PREFACE

"It's always funny until someone gets hurt. Then it's hilarious."
Bill Hicks

Sometimes words are not enough. Other times, pictures are too much.

When I run out of words I use pictures. And when pictures lose their way, I return to words. Poetry comics work because they let the eye roam – making us read and see in competing ways as both text and image operate on different levels of specificity and association.

This collection of poetry comics arises from ideas and lived experience in how communal trauma is comprehended by those subject to it, and the shared silence we learn to maintain.

Each chapter explores dimensions of these experiences. Chapter 1 grounds the reader in the 'estates,' or 'projects' where poverty is rife and where conditions for abuse linger. Chapter 2 unearths the ingredients of trauma in the individual and community. Chapter 3 unfolds a story of perpetrators and silence in 'Mickey and Joan'. In Chapter 4, the after-effects of this unravel and Chapter 5 depicts the further effects of poverty and dissolution of a community's sense of self. The final chapter, 6, takes glimpses from the short lives of my two brothers and the aftermath of their sudden absence.

Russell Evans

chapter one

OCCUPANTS IN SONG

DOORWAY -2°C
when you were given silver blankets
YOU ALWAYS GO MISSING
temperature drop
dependent on a coroner's report
even waiting for for you to call takes it out of me. I to be smashed on and and
Keep a low profile
SITTING, STANDING WAITING... I SAW AND WHAT THEY HEARD OR WHAT THE COPS EVEN IF I'M JUST A WITNESS... THE DOG DRINKS FROM THE SAME PINT GLASS YEH
Febuary
March
April
May
duh... duh... July
A B C D

WHACK
ZOOM
WAIT FOR JOBS.
IT ALL ADDS UP-
CHOLESTEROL, DIAZAPAM
TOOTHACHE, AND
BUY FROM GARY ON FRIDAYS
YEAH.
Mollasses, chicken stock lard
Envelopes
WHITE TILES a boy fell from
the porch of tubular steel
EVERYTHING ON CREDIT
ODDS
Evens
GARY SELLS IT
data compound interest
like a hi-fi at 4 squids a week
or egg for a one-off
payment carry cot self-assembly
chip fryer 2 nights in hospital
(two cars per household)
CASH ONLY

KRAAAAAAAK
CLAP
TICK TICK TICK TICK
BOOM
DON'T STEP OUT OF LINE
DON'T LEAVE ME...
KFC
FROM PSALM 23 TO PAY-PER-VIEW
KRRRR-IK
APPLE
A mourner's party - A TEENAGER'S
DIRTY Funeral one stop to the
takeaway beneath the WHEELS
HIDEAWAY

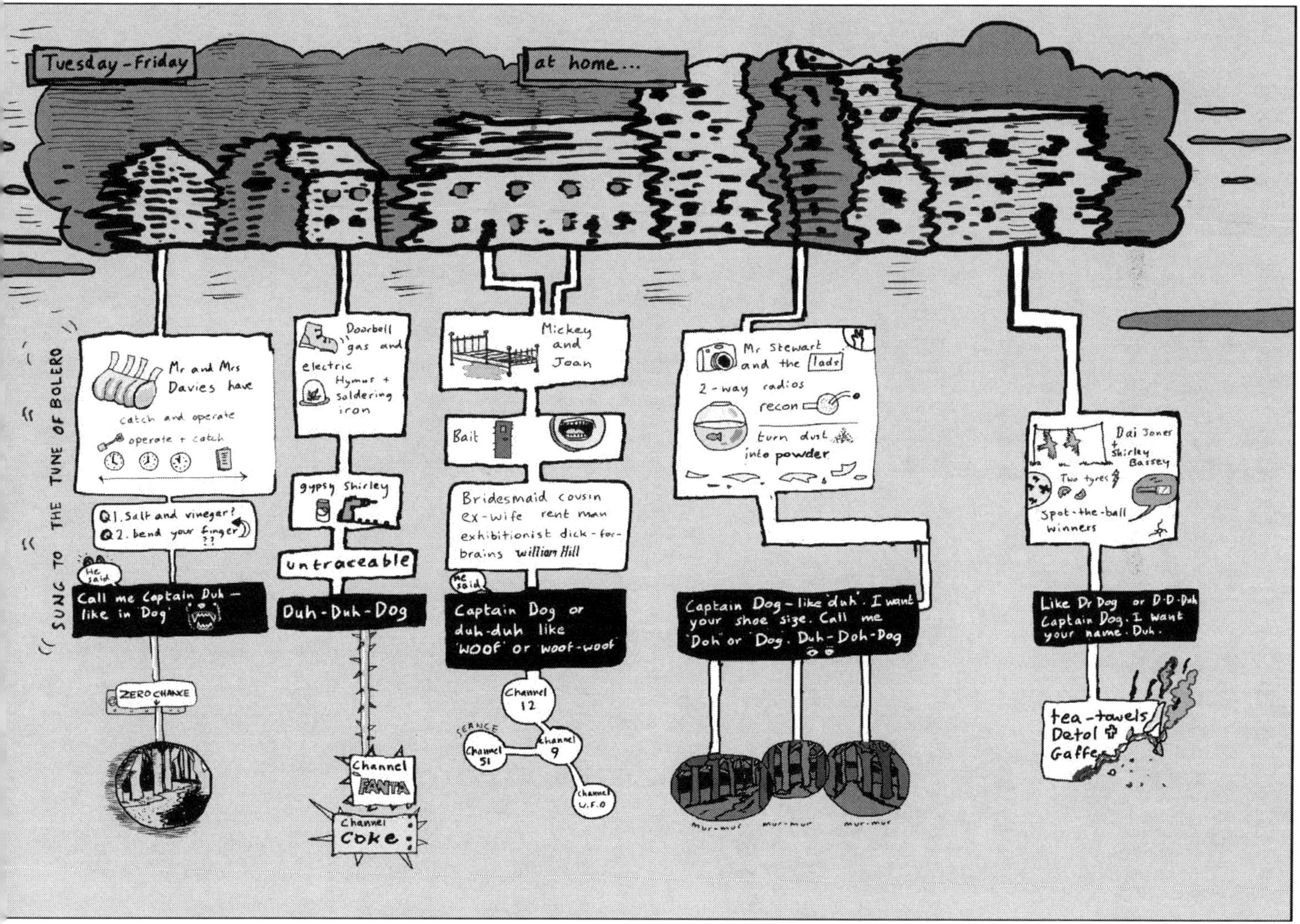

Tuesday-Friday
at home...
SUNG TO THE TUNE OF BOLERO
Mr and Mrs Davies have
catch and operate
operate + catch
Q1. Salt and vinegar?
Q2. bend your finger ??
He said
Call me Captain Duh — like in 'Dog'
ZERO CHANCE
Doorbell gas and electric
Hymus + soldering iron
gypsy Shirley
untraceable
Duh-Duh-Dog
Channel FANTA
Channel Coke
Mickey and Joan
Bait
Bridesmaid cousin ex-wife rent man exhibitionist dick-for-brains William Hill
He said
Captain Dog or duh-duh like 'WOOF' or 'woof-woof'
Channel 12
SEANCE
Channel 51
Channel 9
Channel U.F.O
Mr Stewart and the lads
2-way radios
recon
turn dust into powder
Captain Dog - like 'duh'. I want your shoe size. Call me 'Doh' or 'Dog'. Duh-Doh-Dog
mur-mur
mur-mur
mur-mur
Dai Jones + Shirley Bassey
Two tyres
Spot-the-ball winners
Like Dr Dog or D-D-Duh Captain Dog. I want your name. Duh.
tea-towels
Detol
Gaffe

all day
TO THE TUNE OF STORMY WEATHER
OOFF
ZING
WACK
WHUP
WE JUST PICKED YOU UP YOU LOOK AND TALK LIKE A TOO MUCH
OCCUPANTS 12-91
OCCUPANTS 1-23
THICK MEAT SLICES ON THE SHELF—TIMED EXACTLY (OUCH)
MAKE SURE YOU ASK WHY × 1
WHY SHUE I SAID...
ASK TWICE QUESTIONS 2-9
DON'T BELIEVE QUESTION 2 OR QUESTION 4
OR QUESTION 6—IT'S JUST BLAH
IF YOU GET DETAINED—PUNCH FIRST
LOSE YOUR SIGHT—TAKE A WEEK OFF WORK
SIGN HERE JUST SAY DUH...DUH...

TO THE TUNE OF "WILLOW WEEP FOR ME"
TO THE TUNE OF "SUGAR IN MY BOWL"
hiccup ... hiccup
pst ... psst .... psst ... psst .... pst..
BE THERE— COOK CHIPS AT 2pm
curse hiccup curse hiccup weep hiccup cough psst...
its OK over here over here
supplement vitamins
cook for 5
make excuses
eat cook eat
hear through
DOZY
spill
come away
COOK
SPILL
its alright over here over here it's alright
a separate room with one wall hearing
DUANE EDDY

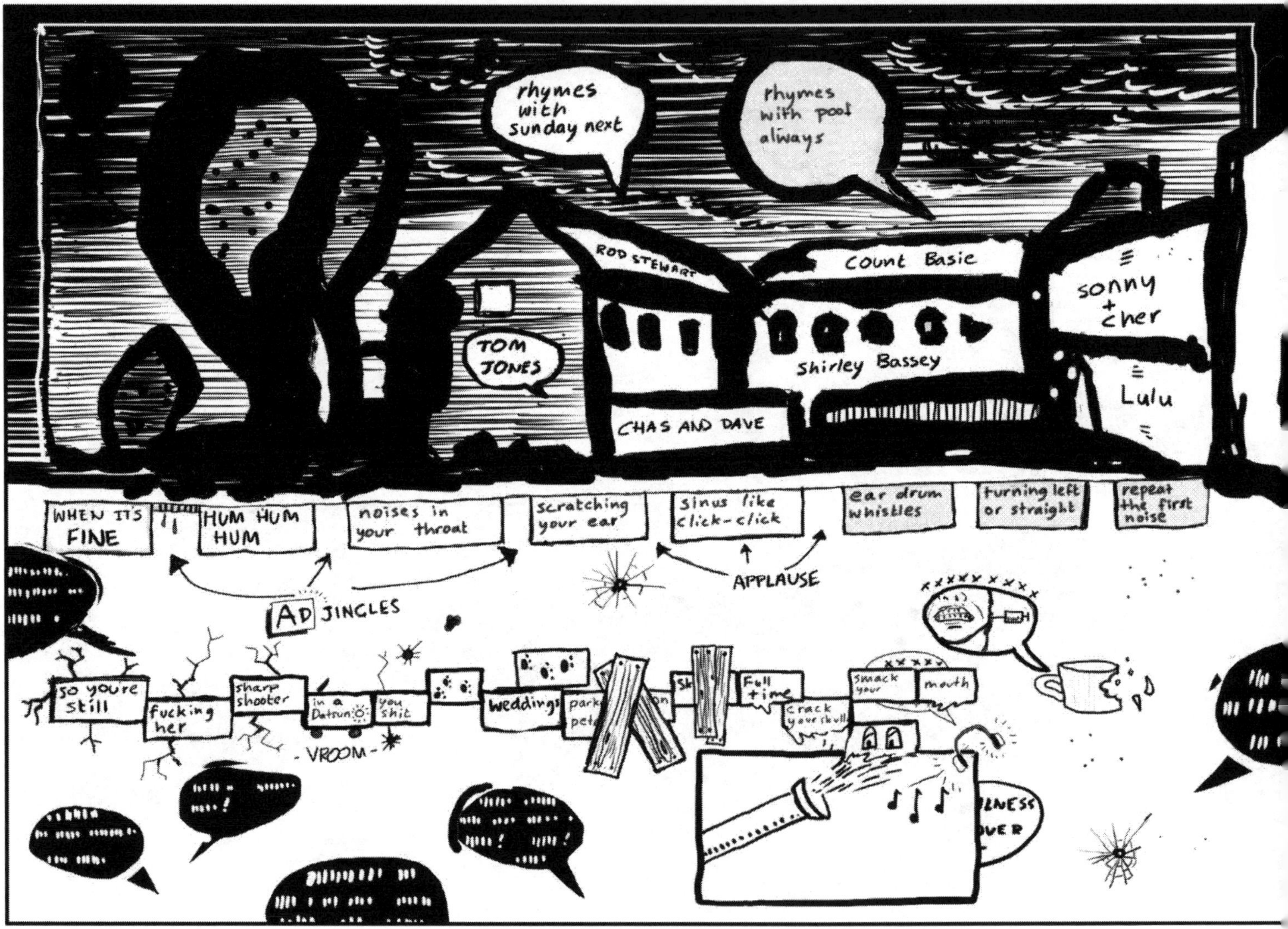

rhymes with sunday next
rhymes with pool always
ROD STEWART
Count Basie
sonny + cher
TOM JONES
Shirley Bassey
Lulu
CHAS AND DAVE
WHEN IT'S FINE
HUM HUM HUM
noises in your throat
scratching your ear
sinus like click-click
ear drum whistles
turning left or straight
repeat the first noise
APPLAUSE
AD JINGLES
so you're still
fucking her
sharp shooter
in a Datsun
you shit
weddings
Full time
crack your skull
smack your
mouth
-VROOM-

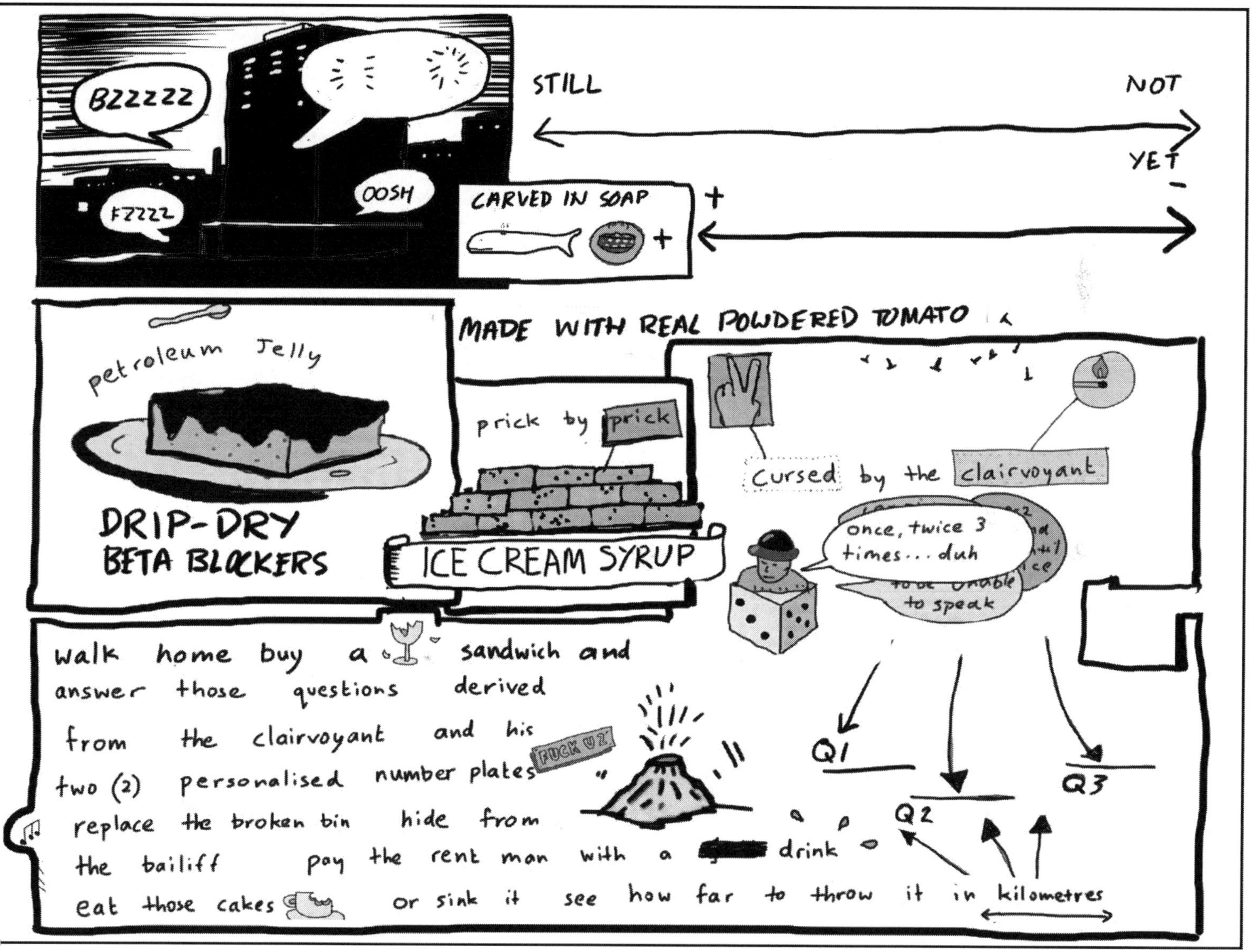
BZZZZZ
FZZZZ
OOSH
STILL
NOT
YET
CARVED IN SOAP
+
+
MADE WITH REAL POWDERED TOMATO
petroleum Jelly
DRIP-DRY
BETA BLOCKERS
prick by prick
ICE CREAM SYRUP
cursed by the clairvoyant
once, twice 3 times... duh
to be unable to speak
walk home buy a sandwich and
answer those questions derived
from the clairvoyant and his
two (2) personalised number plates
FUCK U2
replace the broken bin hide from
the bailiff pay the rent man with a [redacted] drink
eat those cakes or sink it see how far to throw it in kilometres
Q1
Q2
Q3

DING
DING
DING
DING
DING
DING
DING
STEP 1.
AS YOU
ARE GOING
AUSE IT
JUST IS 5
STEP 4
SHWOKKK
I totally get it- the 3am?! wake-up call
THE DOORMAT
SING A SONG TO DO ALL THE NOTES LIKE IT WORKS
BELLOWS AT 2 AM WALK-IN CLINIC DO A TRIPLE TEST FOR KNUCKLE DUSTERS
ALL THE MOVIES EVER SEEN. FEET AND ARMS CHECK YOU KNOW WHAT IT FEELS LIKE TO GO WHACK
Voice #2
Voice #6

SOON
YN FUAN...
Not very hungry
unchanged suitable
BELONGING ON THIS HOUSE
gwaed, braster
Blood, coffee jelly, lard
OIL
SOSPAN
VINEGAR
STILL PLEASE
LARD
JELLY
hair oil 50%
petrol 20%
vaseline 30%
TO THE TUNE OF
WHEN YOU PLAY THE POOLS
SOSPAN FACH
LIKE WHOOSH
I'M NOT HUNGRY
The bailiff wants your **** tea
SOSPAN FACH
WRETCHES
STILL NOT HUNGRY
yn berwi ar yr tân
Boiling by the fire
yr gath wedi sgrapo boy
The cat scratched boy
boy gwas ddim yn iach
and not well
Sospan fawr yn berwi ar y llawr
OOOH!

chapter two

GIFTS ARRIVE ANY TIME

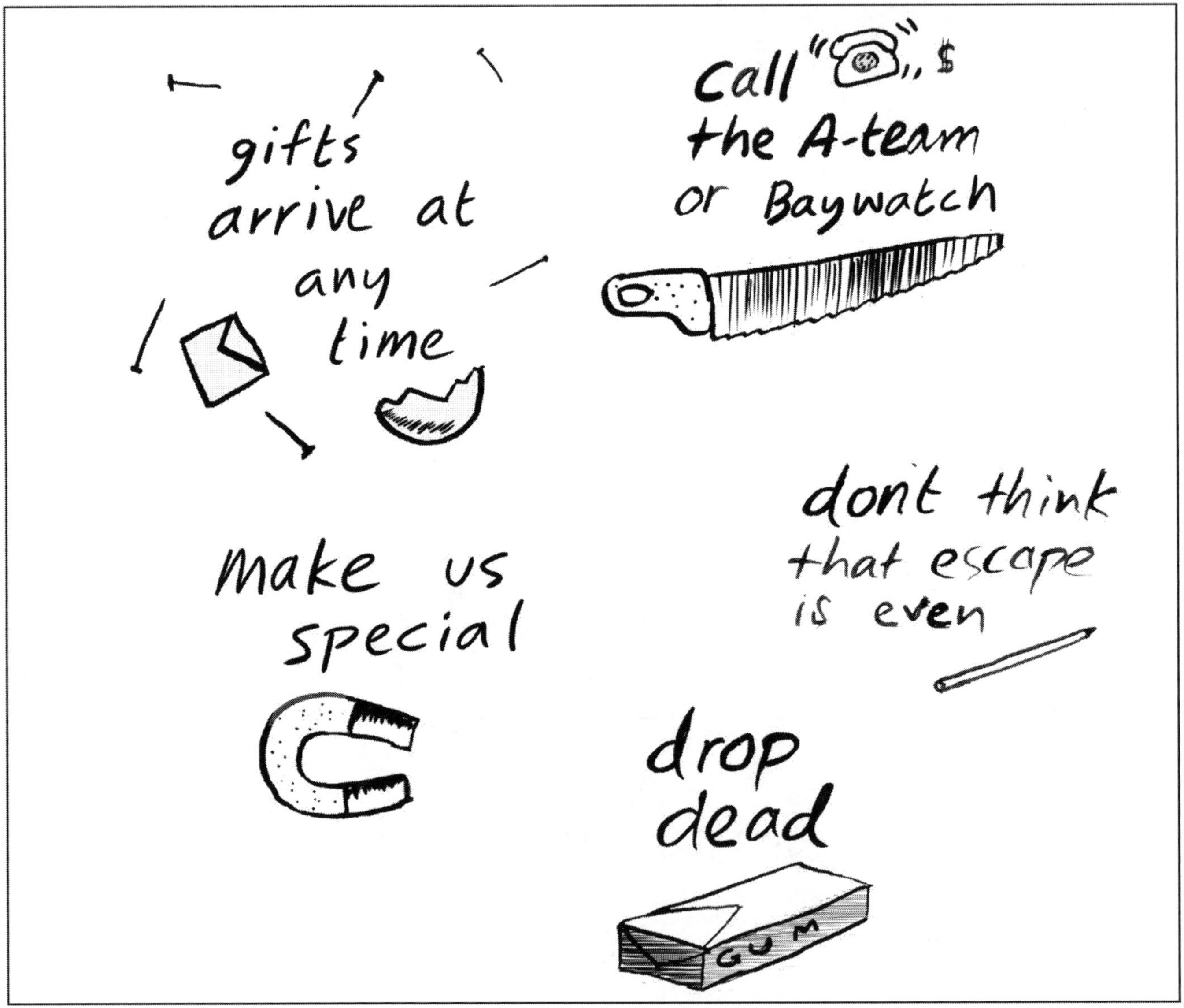
gifts arrive at any time
Call the A-team or Baywatch
$
don't think that escape is even
make us special
drop dead
GUM

show what it takes to score
Twat
dickhead
Don't look
LOOK
sit tight
vodka + coke
Nude
don't cook chips for me
COOK
shat on
Burgled
shitface
Fuckwit

one lane
water
I can drop you just like that
mount snowdon
more books and toys
pay pay
SUGAR
children have a key each

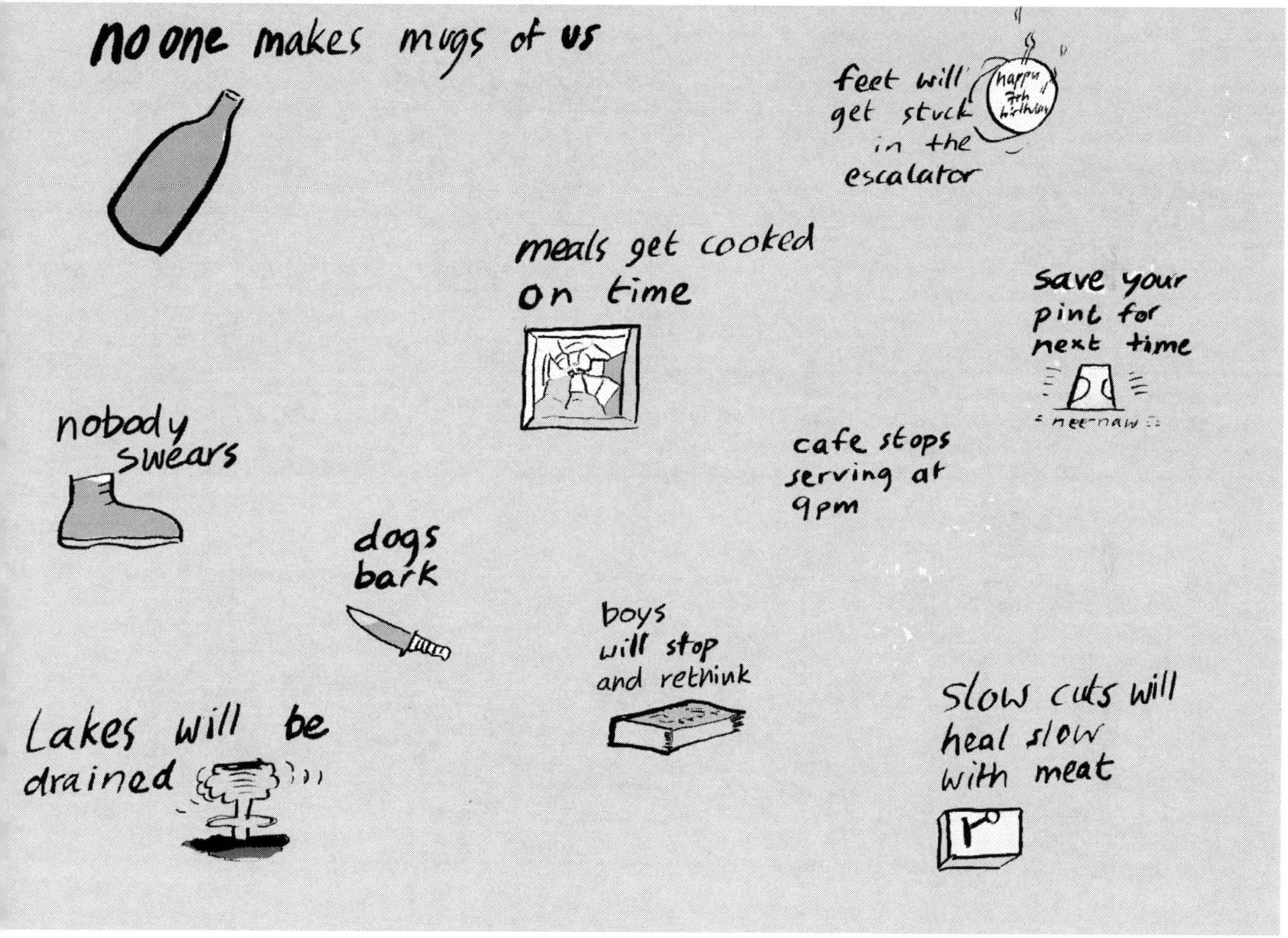
no one makes mugs of us
feet will get stuck in the escalator
happy 7th birthday
meals get cooked on time
save your pint for next time
nee-naw
nobody swears
cafe stops serving at 9pm
dogs bark
boys will stop and rethink
slow cuts will heal slow with meat
Lakes will be drained

we can Make it happen
Read this when I say stop
Cook the same every night
don't make out you knew
Say it's always OK
your fake office chair

google his name
it's obvious in stre t view
choose by not looking
make a fist on the sofa
toast me with thine eyes
make it look accidental how you extract information

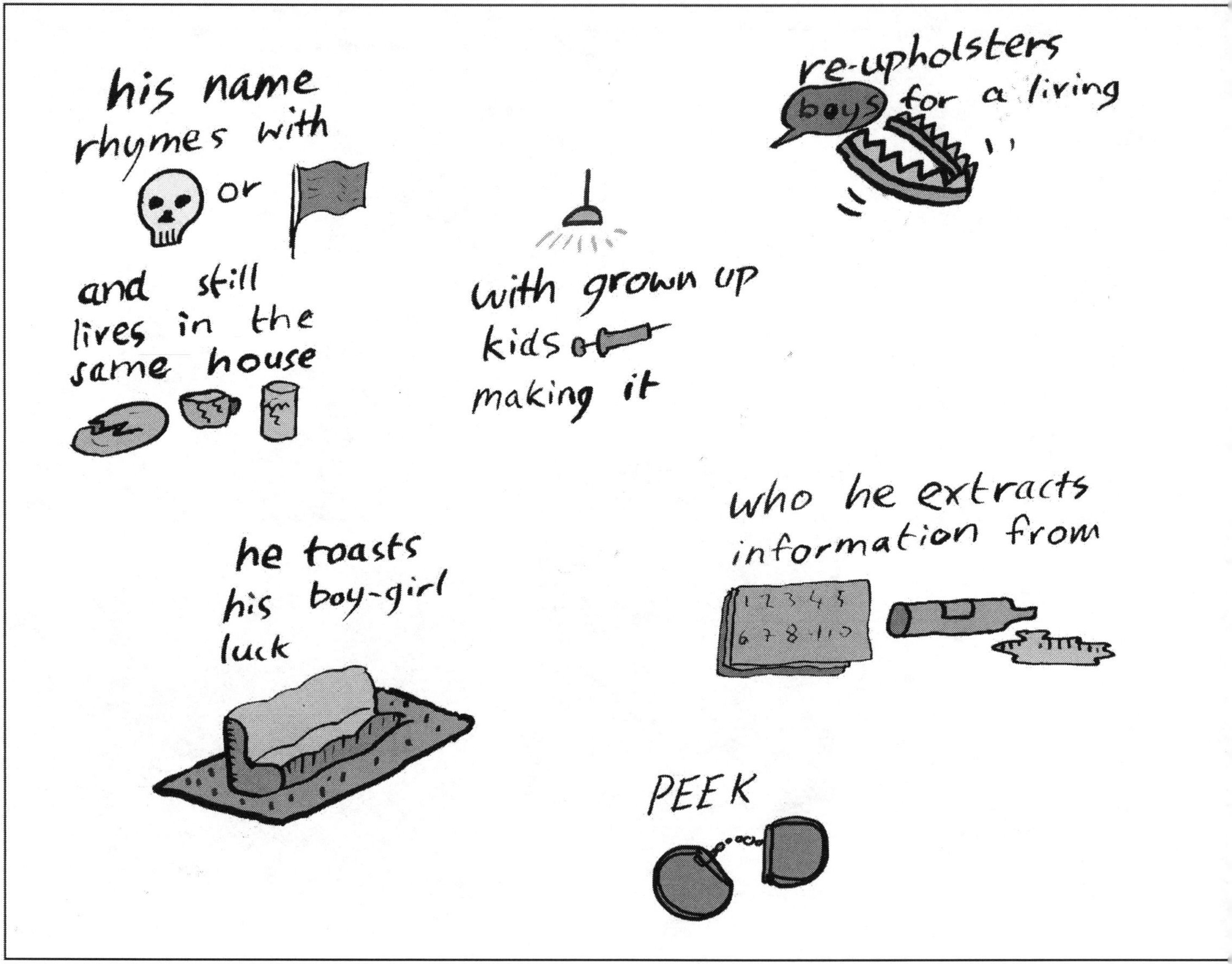
his name rhymes with
or
and still lives in the same house
with grown up kids making it
re-upholsters
boys
for a living
he toasts his boy-girl luck
who he extracts information from
PEEK

FFFZZZZ
THHHWOCKK
"shhhhkraghh"
ka-WHUMPPP
Ksh...
Ksh....
ksh...
Ksh...
va-a-KRRUK
FIZZZZ
FIZZZZ
FIZZZZ

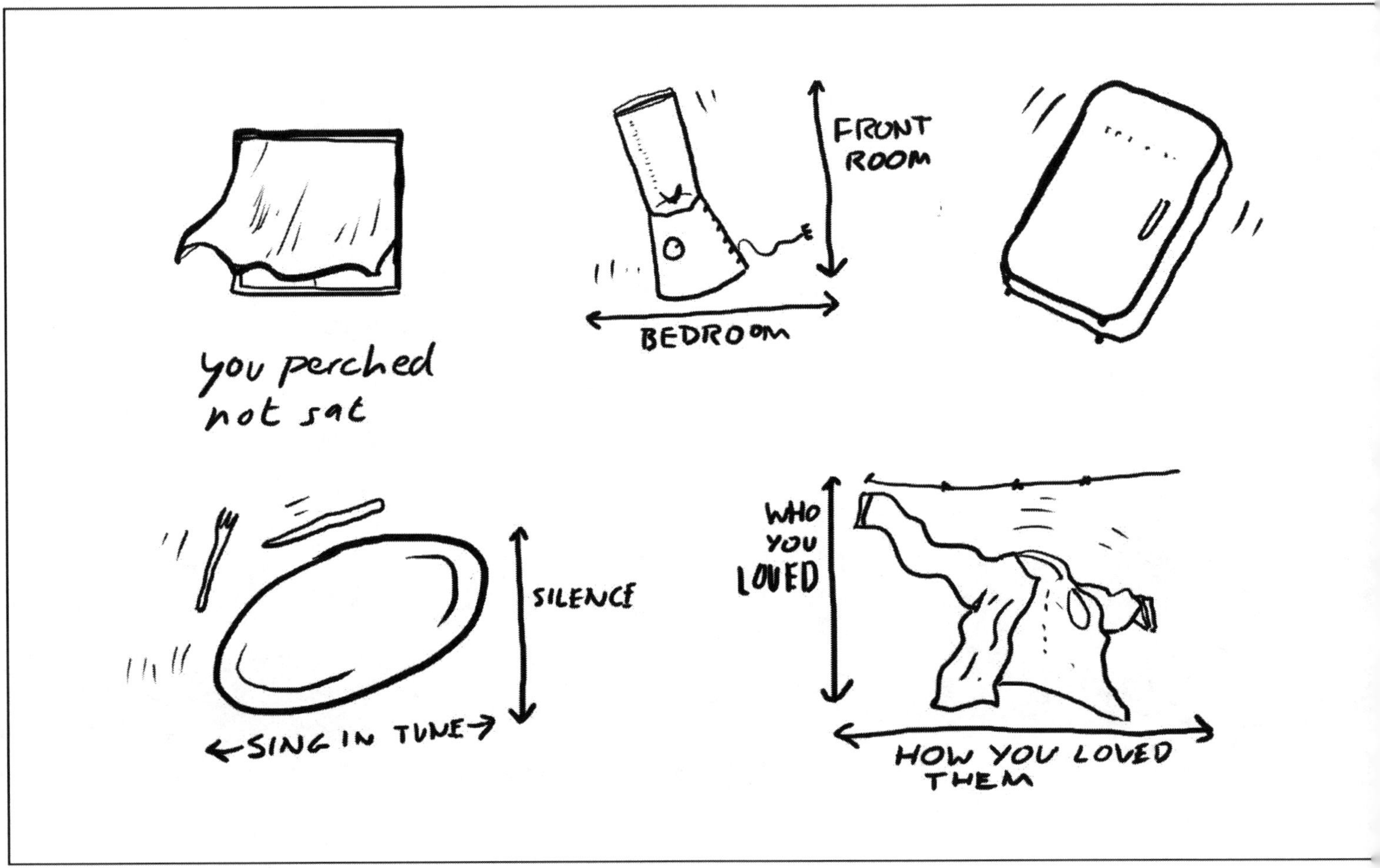
you perched not sat
FRONT ROOM
BEDROOM
SILENCE
SING IN TUNE
WHO YOU LOVED
HOW YOU LOVED THEM

chapter three

IT’S MICKEY AND JOAN

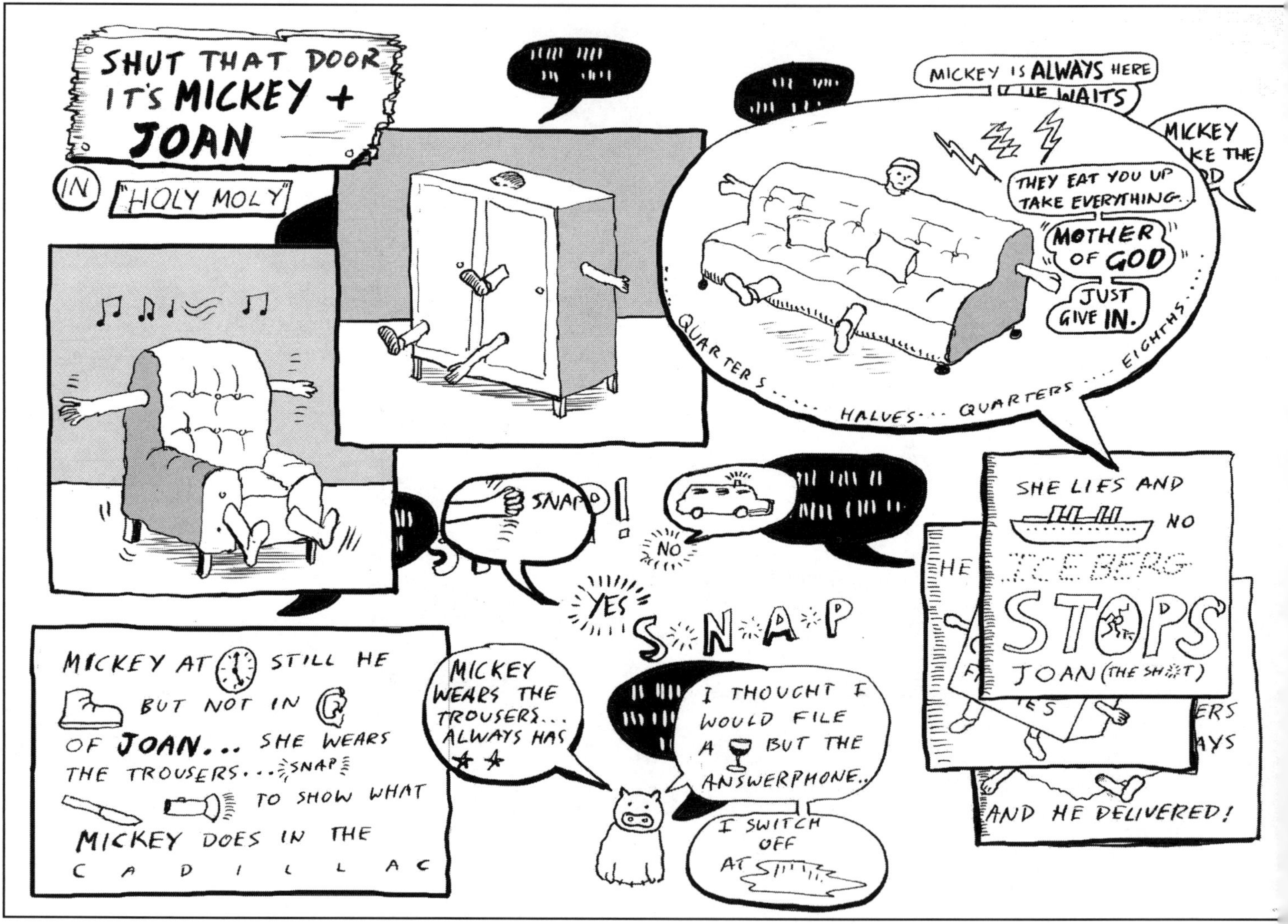
SHUT THAT DOOR IT'S MICKEY + JOAN
IN "HOLY MOLY"
MICKEY IS ALWAYS HERE
THEY EAT YOU UP TAKE EVERYTHING..
"MOTHER OF GOD"
JUST GIVE IN.
QUARTERS..... HALVES... QUARTERS..... EIGHTHS.....
SNAP!
NO
YES
SNAP
SHE LIES AND NO ICEBERG STOPS JOAN (THE SHIT)
AND HE DELIVERED!
MICKEY AT STILL HE BUT NOT IN OF JOAN... SHE WEARS THE TROUSERS... SNAP TO SHOW WHAT MICKEY DOES IN THE CADILLAC
MICKEY WEARS THE TROUSERS... ALWAYS HAS
I THOUGHT I WOULD FILE A BUT THE ANSWERPHONE..
I SWITCH OFF AT

in between
Black 'n' tans
OLD STYLE
in a TV PRESENTER SUIT
NE
NW
E
W
dot dot dot do ren
dash dash dot do ren
he said "call me Captain Duh" just like duh-forgetting. or Dog -
I want your shoe size I want your job I want a ticket to the game tell me some funnies cos I own you. I got a call last night. You don't want to know who.
sideburns
a close attention
to clothes ++ purple
carpets ++ crockery
a house made of dog
teeth + bottle deposit
££
dandelion and burdoch
un-telling under blankets
close scrutiny
Captain Dog - or duh-duh
like it's easy to
remember
WHO YOU CAN TELL:
· LIVERWORT
· THISTLE
· WOOD HAIR MOSS
· WHITE HAIR MOSS
Super-blah blah-blah-
I got you
blah
blah
blah

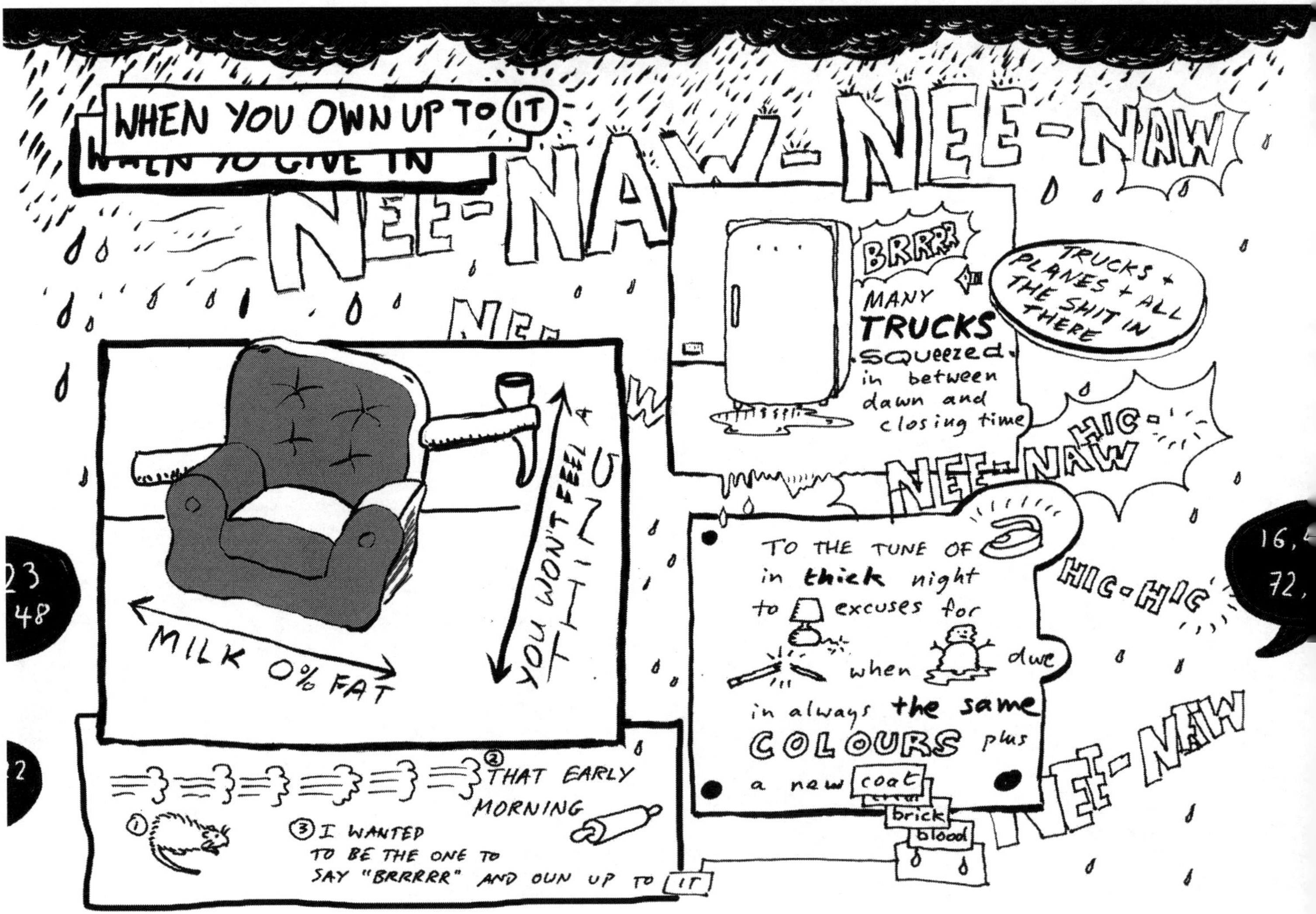
WHEN YOU OWN UP TO IT
WHEN TO GIVE IN
NEE-NAW-NEE-NAW
BRRRR
MANY TRUCKS squeezed in between dawn and closing time
TRUCKS + PLANES + ALL THE SHIT IN THERE
HIC-
NEE-NAW
MILK 0% FAT
YOU WON'T FEEL A THING
TO THE TUNE OF in thick night to excuses for when in always the same COLOURS plus a new coat brick blood
HIG-HIG
NEE-NAW
① ② THAT EARLY MORNING
③ I WANTED TO BE THE ONE TO SAY "BRRRRR" AND OWN UP TO IT

NIGHT (HIC) 2.30am
EMPTY
KNOCK KNOCK!
BELL DON'T WORK (HIC)
Full
HE SAID:
I ONLY TOOK THE DOG OUT
10% bv/ac + DIAZAPAM + WEED TODAY (TA)
COURSE... KNOWING AN END DATE... PSST... PSST... COME CLOSER... PSST... YOUR COLLAR... PSST...
UNTRACED
COLLAR LENGTH
WE FOUND YOU ASLEEP...
PLAIN (PSST) CLOTHES...
Dr DOG
DC/ODETTE/BUTCHER
FUTURE PROOF
A FOIL BLANKET FOR A DOG
DOGS (YEH) WALK THEMSELVES
x2

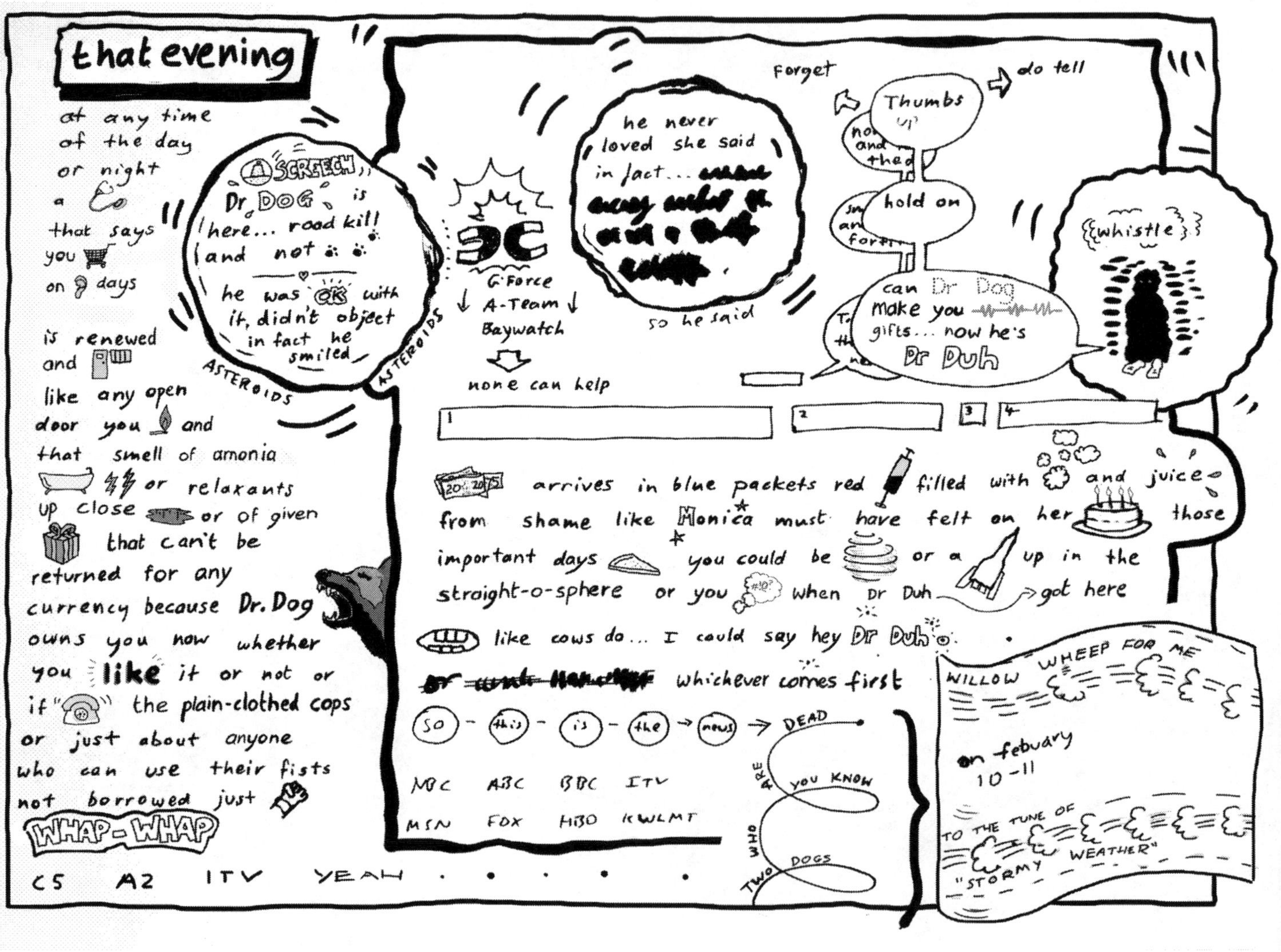

that evening
at any time
of the day
or night
a
that says
you
on days
is renewed
and
like any open
door you and
that smell of amonia
or relaxants
up close or of given
that can't be
returned for any
currency because Dr. Dog
owns you now whether
you like it or not or
if the plain-clothed cops
or just about anyone
who can use their fists
not borrowed just
WHAP-WHAP
C5 A2 ITV YEAH . . . . .
SCREECH
Dr DOG is
here... road kill
and not
he was OK with
it, didn't object
in fact he
smiled
ASTEROIDS
ASTEROIDS
G-Force
A-Team
Baywatch
none can help
he never
loved she said
in fact... [redacted]
so he said
Forget
Thumbs up
do tell
hold on
can Dr Dog
make you
gifts... now he's
Dr Duh
whistle
1
2
3
4
arrives in blue packets red filled with and juice
from shame like Monica must have felt on her those
important days you could be or a up in the
straight-o-sphere or you when Dr Duh got here
like cows do... I could say hey Dr Duh . .
whichever comes first
so - this - is - the - news → DEAD
WHO ARE YOU KNOW
TWO DOGS
NBC ABC BBC ITV
MSN FOX HBO KWLMT
WILLOW WHEEP FOR ME
on febuary
10 -11
TO THE TUNE OF
"STORMY WEATHER"

SO AT TEN PAST THE HOUR THE CAPTAIN SAID "You will never enter the kingdom"... HE JUST CAME OUT...SAID IT...
THAT IS
A SORT OF KNOWLEDGE THAT YOU AND I CAN'T
JUST
2am...
10am
So
SO I SAID... TELL ME THE STORY OF THE DAY TOOK A BIG ... JUST THAT! SO... LATER THERE WAS NOT ... YOU NEVER GUESSED
NEVER ...JUST WITH SO YOU CAN BOTH
SO WE STOOD STILL AND WE WHISTLED
IT WAS SO.... COLD
AT THE SLICES AT STILL. HE DIDN'T KNOW! WHICH DIDN'T ADD UP...

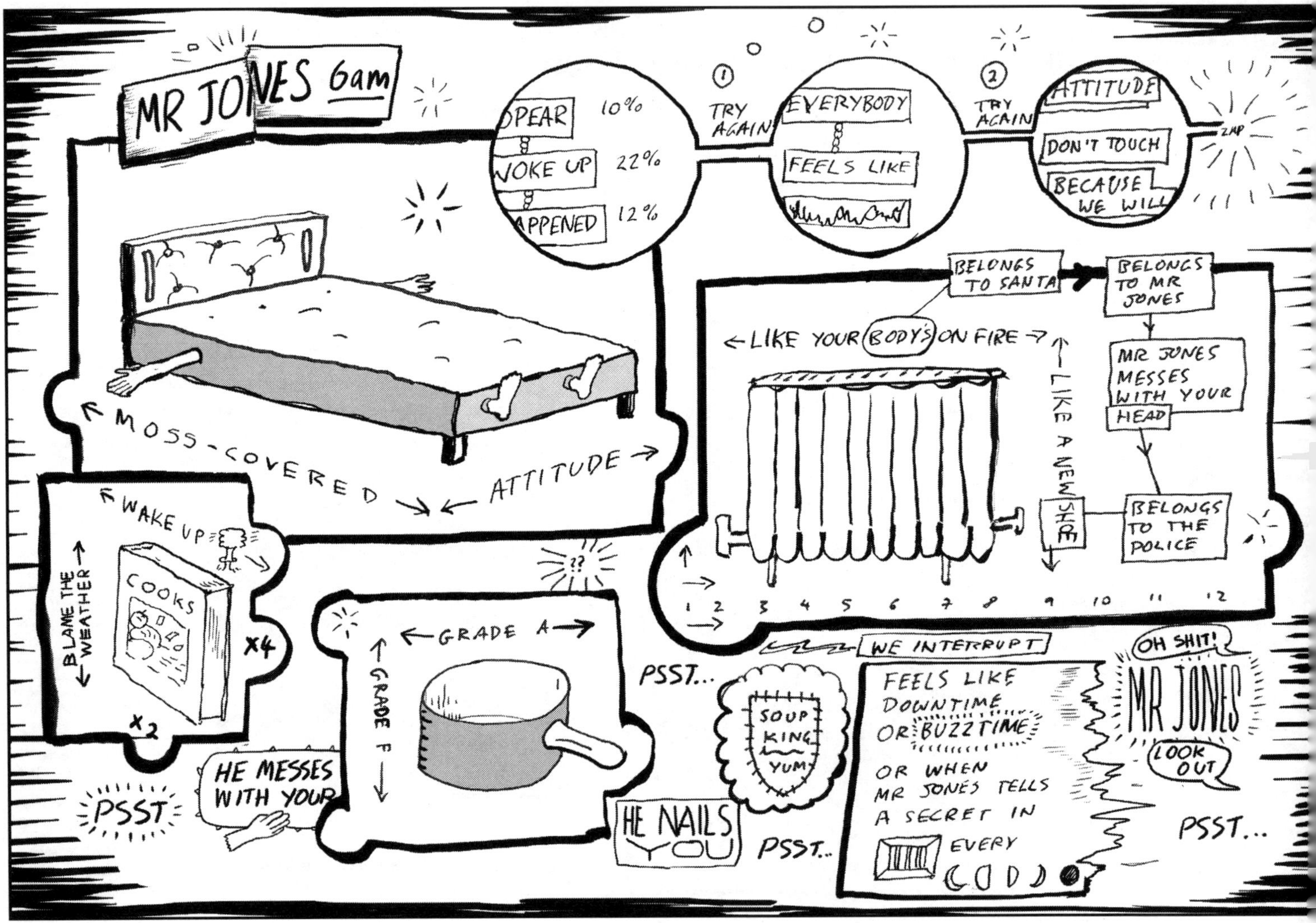
MR JONES 6am
OPEAR 10%
WOKE UP 22%
APPENED 12%
TRY AGAIN
EVERYBODY
FEELS LIKE
TRY AGAIN
ATTITUDE
DON'T TOUCH
BECAUSE WE WILL
ZAP
MOSS-COVERED
ATTITUDE
BELONGS TO SANTA
BELONGS TO MR JONES
LIKE YOUR BODY'S ON FIRE
LIKE A NEW SHOE
MR JONES MESSES WITH YOUR HEAD
BELONGS TO THE POLICE
1 2 3 4 5 6 7 8 9 10 11 12
WAKE UP
BLAME THE WEATHER
COOKS
X4
X2
GRADE A
GRADE F
??
PSST...
WE INTERRUPT
FEELS LIKE DOWNTIME OR BUZZTIME
OR WHEN MR JONES TELLS A SECRET IN
EVERY
OH SHIT!
MR JONES
LOOK OUT
SOUP KING YUM
HE MESSES WITH YOUR
PSST
HE NAILS YOU
PSST...
PSST...

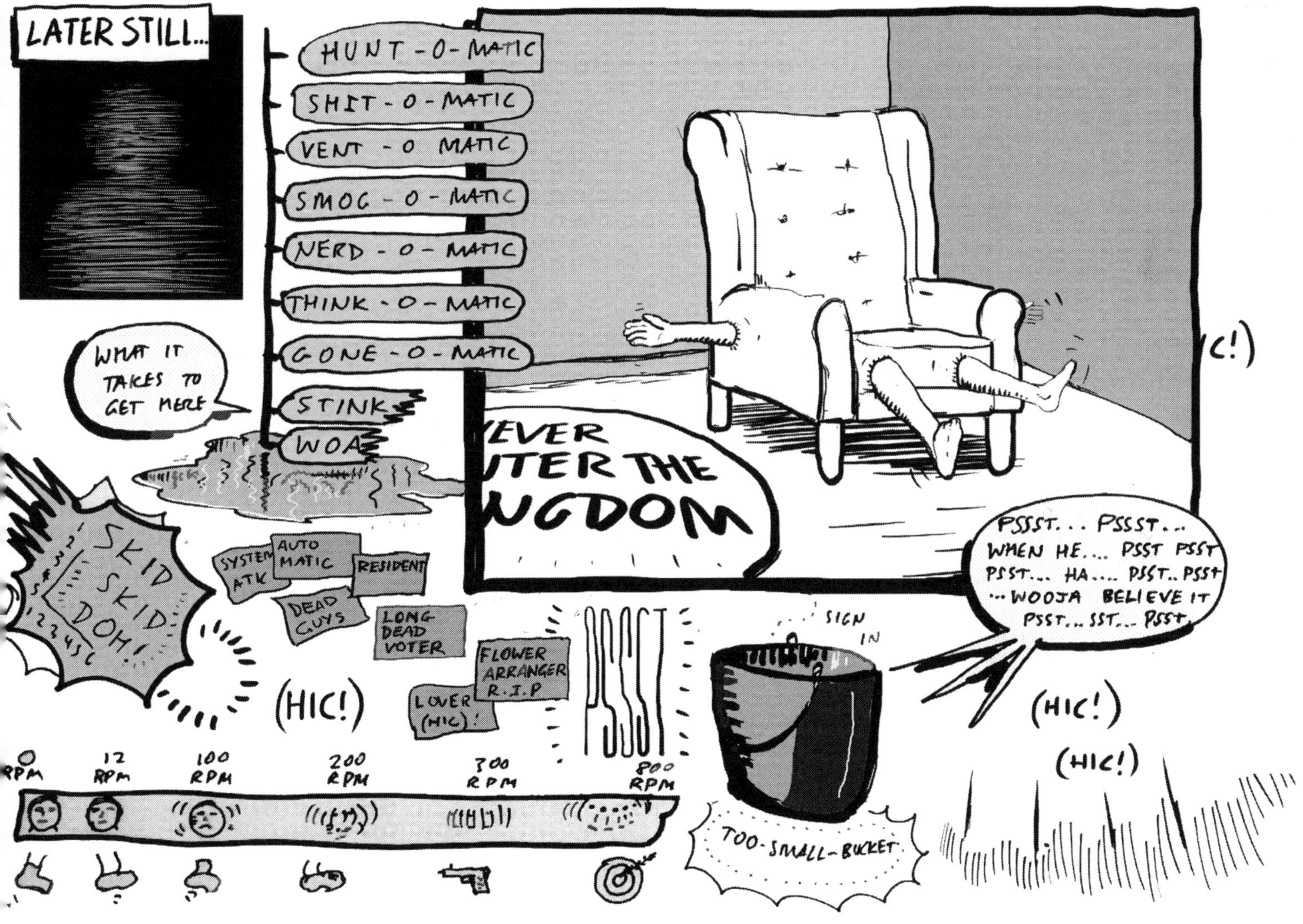
LATER STILL...
HUNT-O-MATIC
SHIT-O-MATIC
VENT-O MATIC
SMOG-O-MATIC
NERD-O-MATIC
THINK-O-MATIC
GONE-O-MATIC
STINK
WOA
WHAT IT TAKES TO GET HERE
EVER
TER THE
GDOM
C!)
SKID SKID DOH!
SYSTEM ATK
AUTO MATIC
RESIDENT
DEAD GUYS
LONG DEAD VOTER
FLOWER ARRANGER R.I.P
LOVER (HIC)
(HIC!)
PSSST
PSSST... PSSST... WHEN HE.... PSST PSST PSST... HA.... PSST.. PSST ...WOOJA BELIEVE IT PSST... SST... PSST.
SIGN IN
(HIC!)
(HIC!)
0 RPM
12 RPM
100 RPM
200 RPM
300 RPM
800 RPM
TOO-SMALL-BUCKET

SOON AFTER...
Walk in through any door
REMOVE YOUR SHOES
SMILE
NOW STAB · AND STAB AGAIN
NOW WIPE CLEAN
A MISH MASH OF
Like a double shot
A SUDDEN HIT TO THE
EEAARGH
A QUICK NEUTRALISING OF THE MOMENT
FULL
HALF FULL
HALF EMPTY
EMPTY
DUH DUH DUH
Anyone steps near - tell us NOW
ALWAYS MAKE SURE YOU GET A NUMBER
2/4 TIME
DUH DUH DUH DUH DUH DUH DUH
'Feet head shoes, smell of
DUH DUH DUH DUH DUH
DUH DUH
CRAARK
CRIKK

chapter four

YOU'RE WITH ME NOW

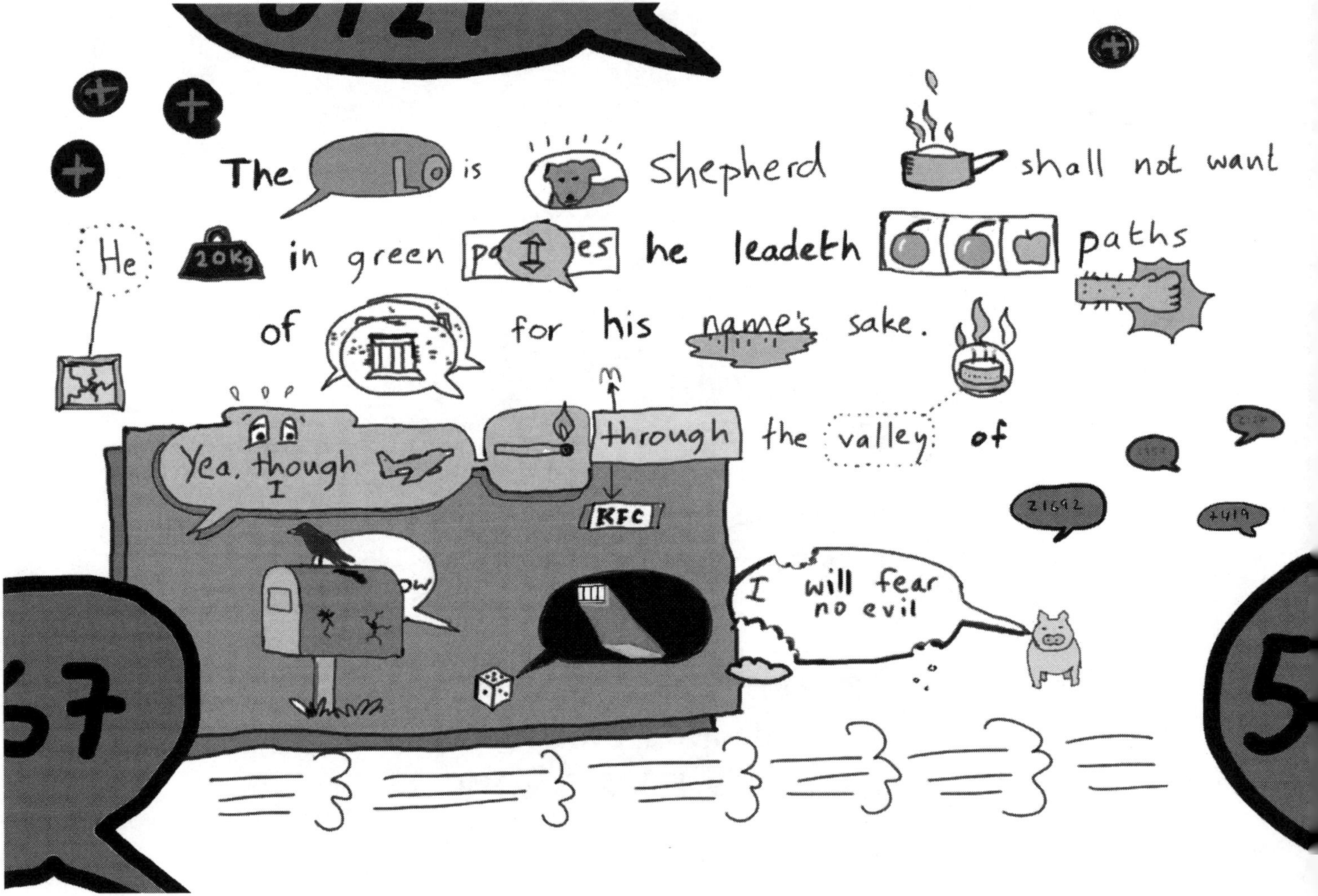
The
LO
is
Shepherd
shall not want
He
20Kg
in green
pa
es
he leadeth
paths
of
for his
name's
sake.
Yea, though I
through
the
valley
of
KFC
ow
I will fear
no evil
21692
7419
67
5

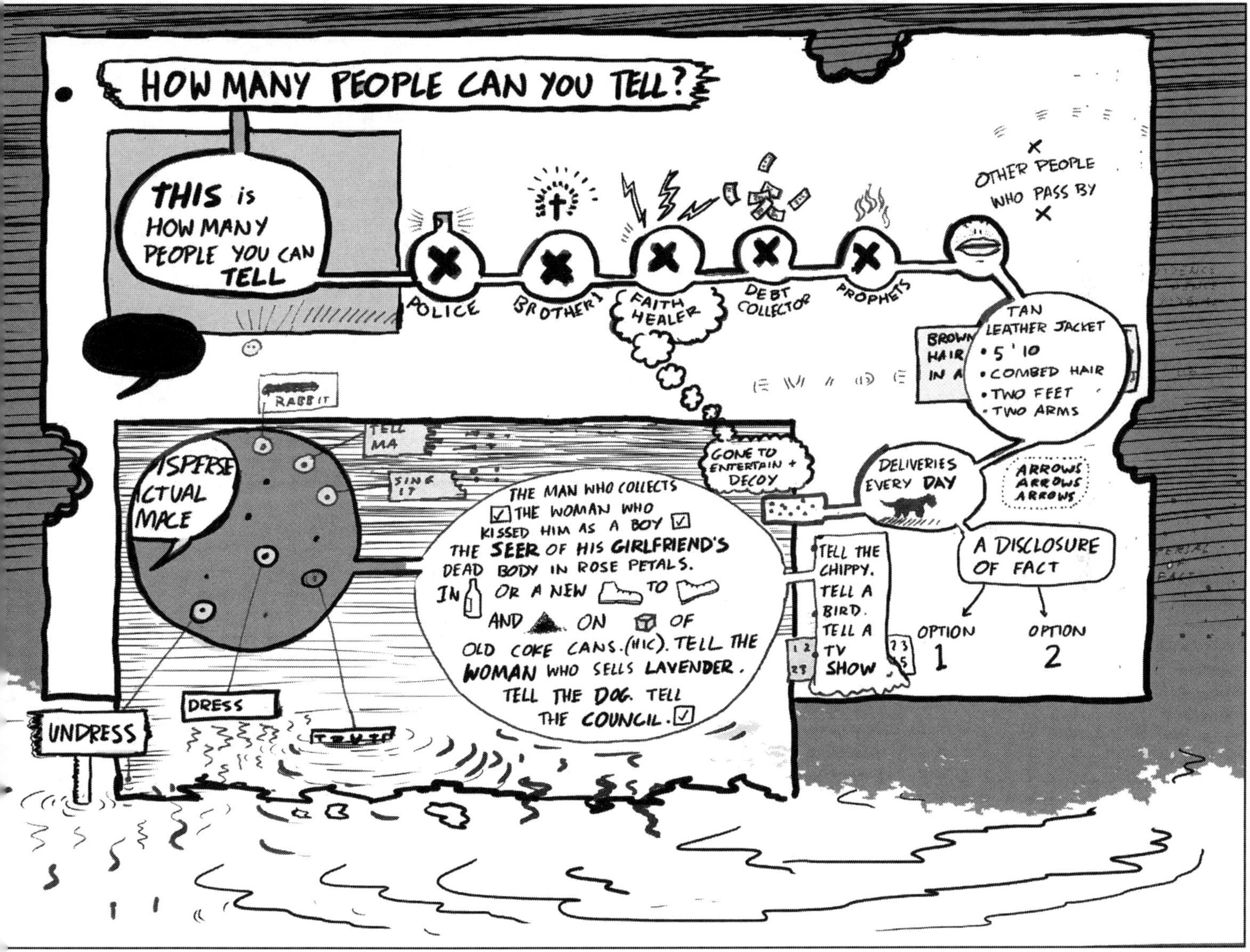
HOW MANY PEOPLE CAN YOU TELL?
THIS is HOW MANY PEOPLE YOU CAN TELL
POLICE
BROTHER
FAITH HEALER
DEBT COLLECTOR
PROPHETS
OTHER PEOPLE WHO PASS BY
TAN LEATHER JACKET
• 5 ' 10
• COMBED HAIR
• TWO FEET
• TWO ARMS
BROWN HAIR IN A
RABBIT
TELL MA
SING IT
ISPERSE CTUAL MACE
GONE TO ENTERTAIN + DECOY
DELIVERIES EVERY DAY
ARROWS ARROWS ARROWS
THE MAN WHO COLLECTS ☑ THE WOMAN WHO KISSED HIM AS A BOY ☑ THE SEER OF HIS GIRLFRIEND'S DEAD BODY IN ROSE PETALS. IN OR A NEW TO AND ON OF OLD COKE CANS.(HIC). TELL THE WOMAN WHO SELLS LAVENDER. TELL THE DOG. TELL THE COUNCIL. ☑
TELL THE CHIPPY. TELL A BIRD. TELL A TV SHOW
A DISCLOSURE OF FACT
OPTION 1
OPTION 2
DRESS
UNDRESS
TRUTH

HEY KID!
BLAM - BLAM
WHEN YOU WOKE UP
PISSED
YUP
SO TO THE DOCTOR SOLD
20
GREEN YEAH YEAH SHIELD
RING
DADS GONE TO ICELAND
NO NEED FOR ANY EMBALMER
SHE WAS ASLEEP
BLAM
AT THE
THIS MUCH
THIS MUCH
THIS MUCH
HEY KID.. HOW ABOUT JUST YOU AND ME
HOPE
SHOPS
LORD OF ALL SHIT
PORK SCRATCHINGS
CLICK
CLICK
I SAW YOU. WE BELONG TOGETHER
BIN MEN
PAEDO
DOCTORS
HIC-HIC
POSH GEEZER
CAN YOU TAKE ME BACK TO LAST YEAR
TANGLED MIS-STATEMENT
HIC, HIC
TICK
M CHARLUS VS THE VIOLINIST
TICK
HEY KID!
WOKE UP!

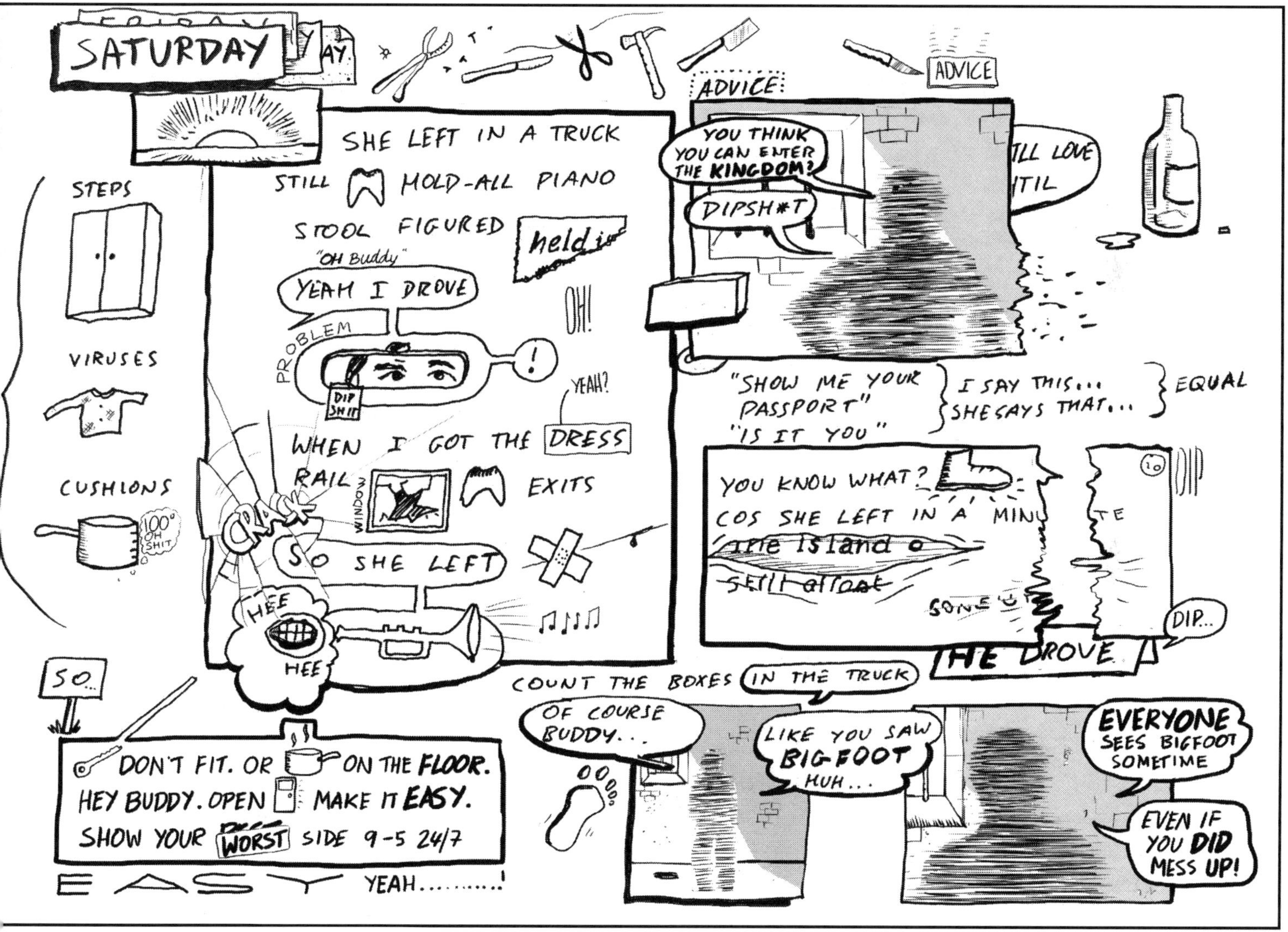

SATURDAY
ADVICE
STEPS
VIRUSES
CUSHIONS
100° OH SHIT
SHE LEFT IN A TRUCK
STILL HOLD-ALL PIANO
STOOL FIGURED
held
"OH Buddy"
YEAH I DROVE
OH!
PROBLEM
!
DIP SHIT
YEAH?
WHEN I GOT THE DRESS
RAIL WINDOW EXITS
CRACK
SO SHE LEFT
HEE HEE
ADVICE
YOU THINK YOU CAN ENTER THE KINGDOM?
DIPSH*T
ILL LOVE
TIL
"SHOW ME YOUR PASSPORT"
"IS IT YOU"
I SAY THIS...
SHE SAYS THAT...
EQUAL
YOU KNOW WHAT?
COS SHE LEFT IN A MIN
the island
still afloat
TE
DIP
DIP...
HE DROVE
SO...
COUNT THE BOXES IN THE TRUCK
OF COURSE BUDDY...
LIKE YOU SAW BIGFOOT HUH...
EVERYONE SEES BIGFOOT SOMETIME
EVEN IF YOU DID MESS UP!
DON'T FIT. OR ON THE FLOOR.
HEY BUDDY. OPEN MAKE IT EASY.
SHOW YOUR WORST SIDE 9-5 24/7
EASY YEAH..........!

ALWAYS
NEVER
TELL ME
THE STORY
HOW MOTHER GAVE US TO THE PAEDOPHILES
DOCTOR •
MAN IN WHITE •
TWO DOLLARS •
ALWAYS KNOWS WHAT TO SAY
Come always where? Ok!
Und to anot 18...
WALL
12 18 19
ALLUMINUM
ALLOY
IRON
ARSENIC
SORRY
NO POINTS
NIL POINT
ZERO PANT

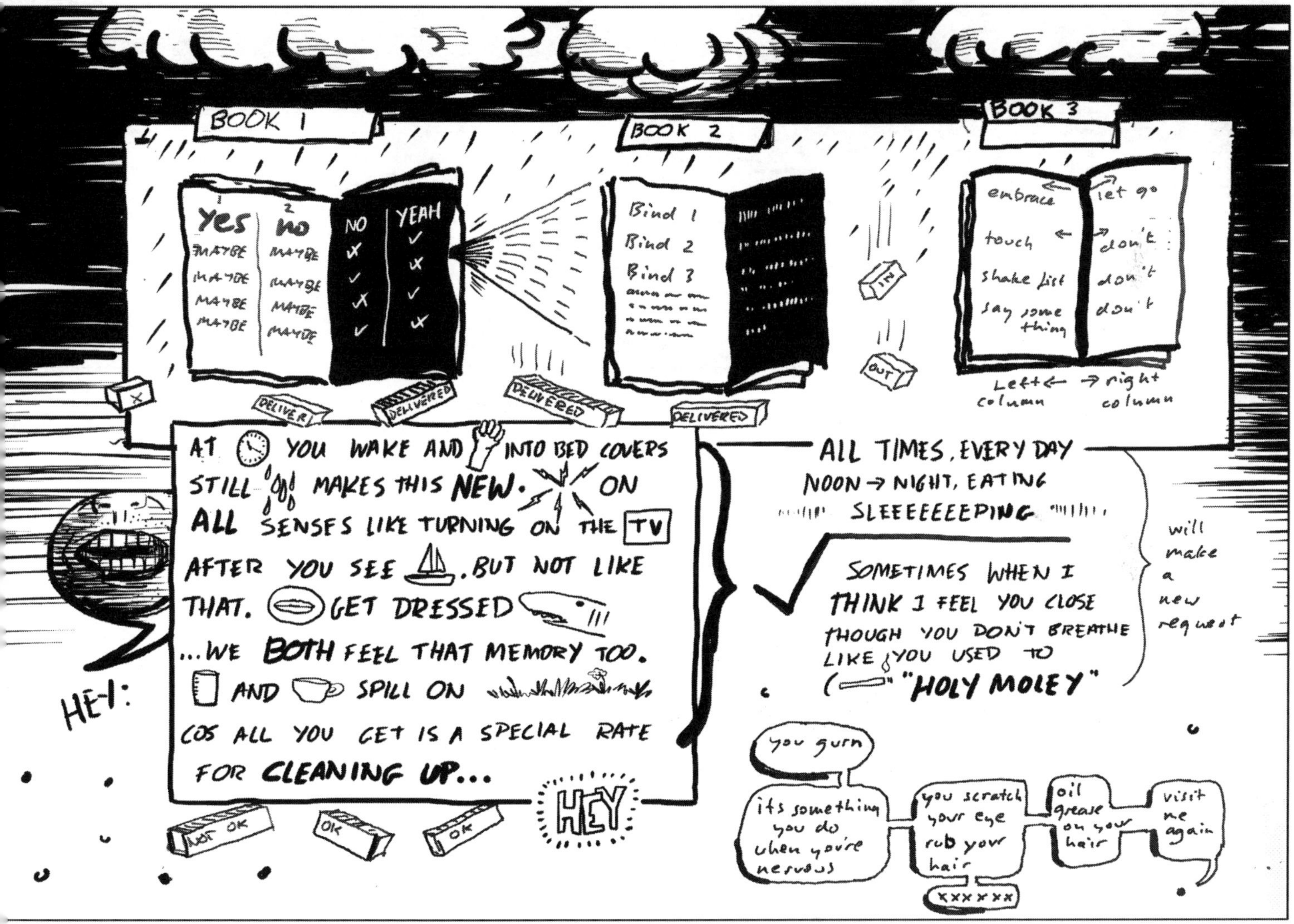
BOOK 1
BOOK 2
BOOK 3
1 YES 2 NO
MAYBE MAYBE
MAYBE MAYBE
MAYBE MAYBE
MAYBE MAYBE
NO YEAH
Bind 1
Bind 2
Bind 3
embrace let go
touch don't
shake fist don't
say some thing don't
IN
OUT
Left column
right column
X
DELIVERED
DELIVERED
DELIVERED
DELIVERED
AT YOU WAKE AND INTO BED COVERS STILL MAKES THIS NEW. ON ALL SENSES LIKE TURNING ON THE TV AFTER YOU SEE . BUT NOT LIKE THAT. GET DRESSED ...WE BOTH FEEL THAT MEMORY TOO. AND SPILL ON COS ALL YOU GET IS A SPECIAL RATE FOR CLEANING UP...
ALL TIMES, EVERY DAY NOON → NIGHT, EATING SLEEEEEEEPING
SOMETIMES WHEN I THINK I FEEL YOU CLOSE THOUGH YOU DON'T BREATHE LIKE YOU USED TO "HOLY MOLEY"
will make a new request
HEY:
HEY
NOT OK
OK
OK
you gurn
its something you do when you're nervous
you scratch your eye rub your hair
xxxxxx
oil grease on your hair
visit me again

KA-CHUNK
KA-CHUK
KA-CHUK
WHAP-WAP
WHAP.
MUH MM - DUH
KA-MA-MA
DUH-DUH-DUH
DUH DUH DUH
MA MA MA
MA MA MA
KA KAH KAH
DUH DUH
DUH DUH
DUH
DUH DUH..
MUH MUH
DUH DUH
DUH
MUH MUH
1 DUH DUH DUH MUH MUH... DUH MUH DUH DUH DUH...DUH.. DUH
DUH MUH DUH DUH MUH DUH DUH DUH.
2 MUH MUH DUH DUH DUH DUH MUH MUH MUH MUH DUH DUH
3 DUH DUH DUH DUH

IF YOU TELL WHO
ASLEEP
CHOMP-CHOMP
RAINY DAY MUSIC
ON ANY DAY... AT
OR THIS OR T
BOOM BOOM
CID
IF YOU REMEMBER ANYTHING
1 FACIAL HAIR
2 EYE COLOUR
3 GAIT
TALL OR MAY BE THIN
BRRR...
IF
AFTER NOT BEING AT HOME
OR
BUT STUPID O'CLOCK
BZZZ BZZZ
AND
KA-THUMP
RING-RING
RING
K-K-K-K
PINCH ME
HE ALWAYS LOOKED IN THROUGH WITH
BRRR... BRR...
TOUCH
TEN O'CLOCK
PSSST... PSSST..
PSS.... PSSST..... PSST
WHOOPS
HA HA HA
USE IT
BANG
PSST... PSST....
simple time
ITS YOU+ME
YOU+
THAT WAS ALL I HEARD
YEAH
YEAH-YEAH
ZIP IT
WUMP
RING-RING
RING-RING
HE WATCHED LIKE
CHOMP CHOMP
SHITFACE
KFC
HE LETS HIMSELF IN THRU'
DON'T SAY THE ANSWER
BRRRRINGG! - BRRRRINNNG!
RING-RING
PSSSSTTTT...
PSSSST...
YOU LOSE
RING RING
CLICK
HE CHARMS
WELC AME
RING-RING!
RING
PSST... PSSST... PSS...
ZIP
BITE HERE
SHOW YOUR FEET YOUR AND
TWIST
BZZZ
KA-CHUNK
CODE
OUCH OUCH OUCH OUCH
RING-RING
ZIP IT ZIP
ZONE 1
ZONE 2
NOW
WE CAN SLEEP
YOU LOSE
BBBRINGG!.....

Saturday–
'the soothsayer'
August 17
June 11
Nov 23
Sept 21
May 14
@
!
!
then...
the house is broken like a zipper
he says
I see things
he says
like scary shit people who died
you got trouble here
he says
huh?
so £££ and £ and £ and then £
££££
step on that step
not that one!
That has bad luck
that picture of HOUDINI cursed your house...
Duh 1
Duh 2
Duh 3
Duh 4
ABC
PSST!
you're with me now
5p for guaranteed release
←miles and miles→
Jan.
March
STILL FOREARM
ADDED
PSST... SO HE.. ...PSST..PSST
...AND THEY... PSST.. PSST... YEH.
His car number plate cost £FUCK KNOWS
SST

HA HA Ha Ha
BE VERY STILL . IN TIME THINGS CALM DOWN IN 2's AND 3's
and
always end.. people leave
in , stalling, leaving
or hailing
still again. Like stones
pull on shoelaces tight.
Monday and friday
make a double helping
SIGH YOU JUST WAIT
MAKE IT LOOK EASY
129 LLANEDE
22 COE-Y-GORES
(NO GO FOR TAXIS)
2 months
a killing @!#☆?!!☆
or clean up with
or a
1
SIGH
KNOW THAT WITH
2
HA, YOU MAKE IT LOOK
SIGH
HIC

chapter five

CUT OFF YOUR CREDIT

1
YEAH cut off your credit
2
AT
IF IT
POSSIBLE
Home by nightfall
3
ZZZZIP
2/4 TIME
put your toes in sockets
PRETEND
NO BODY ODOUR NO VOICE NO TAX RETURN NO DICK
~~Decipher~~ untangle or maybe just do nothing...
smell sweetly by soap TOOTHPASTE AND SHAMPOO...
OR FORGET TO WASH
PRESS YOUR TROUSERS DON'T STEP ON WORMS BE NICE DON'T TALK
BUCKETS, POTATOES CASHED-IN RENT BOOK OR FIND
OVER 3 YEARS
LEECHED CENTRAL NERVOUS SYSTEM

ALWAYS AT 2a.m
BRRRR
BRRR
GIVE UP
SIZE
10
SHOES
CALL YOUR MA
CALL 999
BLEEP BLEEP
HOLD
TIGHT
HOLD TIGHTER
HOLD TIGHTER
BRRR
REPORT THOSE CONVERSATIONS WITH PEOPLE WHO SCARED OF TALKING AND WON'T REPORT ANYTHING
BRRR
$
25
25

your voice
inherited from 6 generations
a child I was a footprint on my own thigh "Pretend" to love
a claw streak of bare bone
candy crush
bones inherit $
DON'T EAT
EAT
MON
TUES
FORGET
EAT FRIES
BIG
DE-LOUSED
Love
HATE
SKINNED
EAT
LOVE
LOVE
CUT
LOVE
STAB
HOLLOW BONE MARROW
tell me my teeth look like yours

GET TO KNOW THE KING "OF THIEVES"
- DEEP FRY -
- STAND TALL -
- SAY YEAH -
DON'T STARE
STAMP, STAMP
STAMP, STAMP
SEEM LIKE YOU MEAN BUSINESS
in the wash
it looks bright
CHICKEN VS PIE VS BURGERS ALL NIGHT

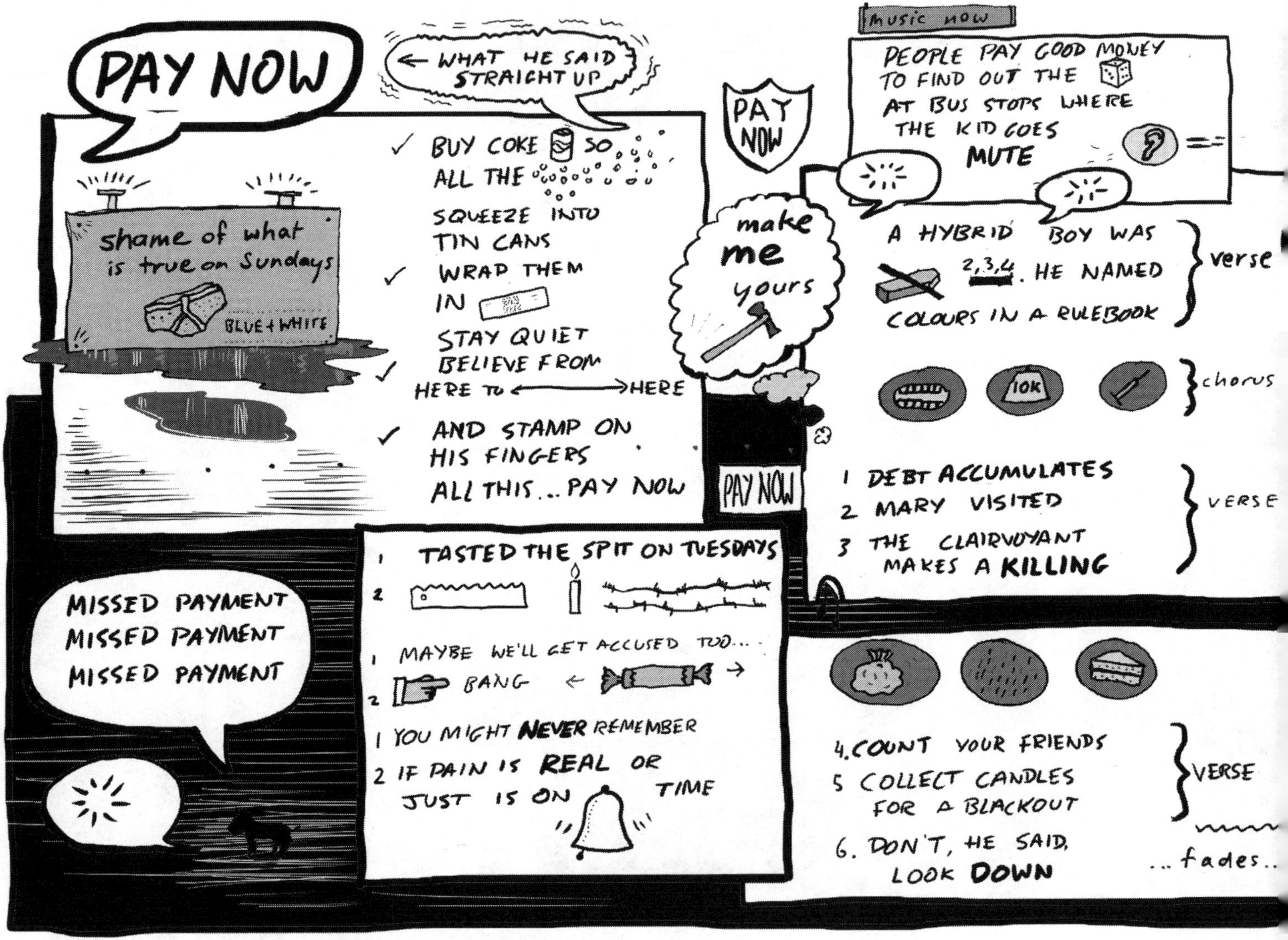

PAY NOW
← WHAT HE SAID STRAIGHT UP
✓ BUY COKE SO ALL THE
SQUEEZE INTO TIN CANS
✓ WRAP THEM IN
STAY QUIET BELIEVE FROM
✓ HERE TO ⟷ HERE
✓ AND STAMP ON HIS FINGERS
ALL THIS... PAY NOW
shame of what is true on Sundays
BLUE + WHITE
PAY NOW
make me yours
PAY NOW
MUSIC NOW
PEOPLE PAY GOOD MONEY TO FIND OUT THE AT BUS STOPS WHERE THE KID GOES MUTE
A HYBRID BOY WAS 2,3,4. HE NAMED COLOURS IN A RULEBOOK
verse
10K
chorus
1 DEBT ACCUMULATES
2 MARY VISITED
3 THE CLAIRVOYANT MAKES A KILLING
VERSE
1 TASTED THE SPIT ON TUESDAYS
2
1 MAYBE WE'LL GET ACCUSED TOO...
2 BANG ← →
1 YOU MIGHT NEVER REMEMBER
2 IF PAIN IS REAL OR JUST IS ON TIME
MISSED PAYMENT
MISSED PAYMENT
MISSED PAYMENT
4. COUNT YOUR FRIENDS
5 COLLECT CANDLES FOR A BLACKOUT
VERSE
6. DON'T, HE SAID, LOOK DOWN
... fades ..

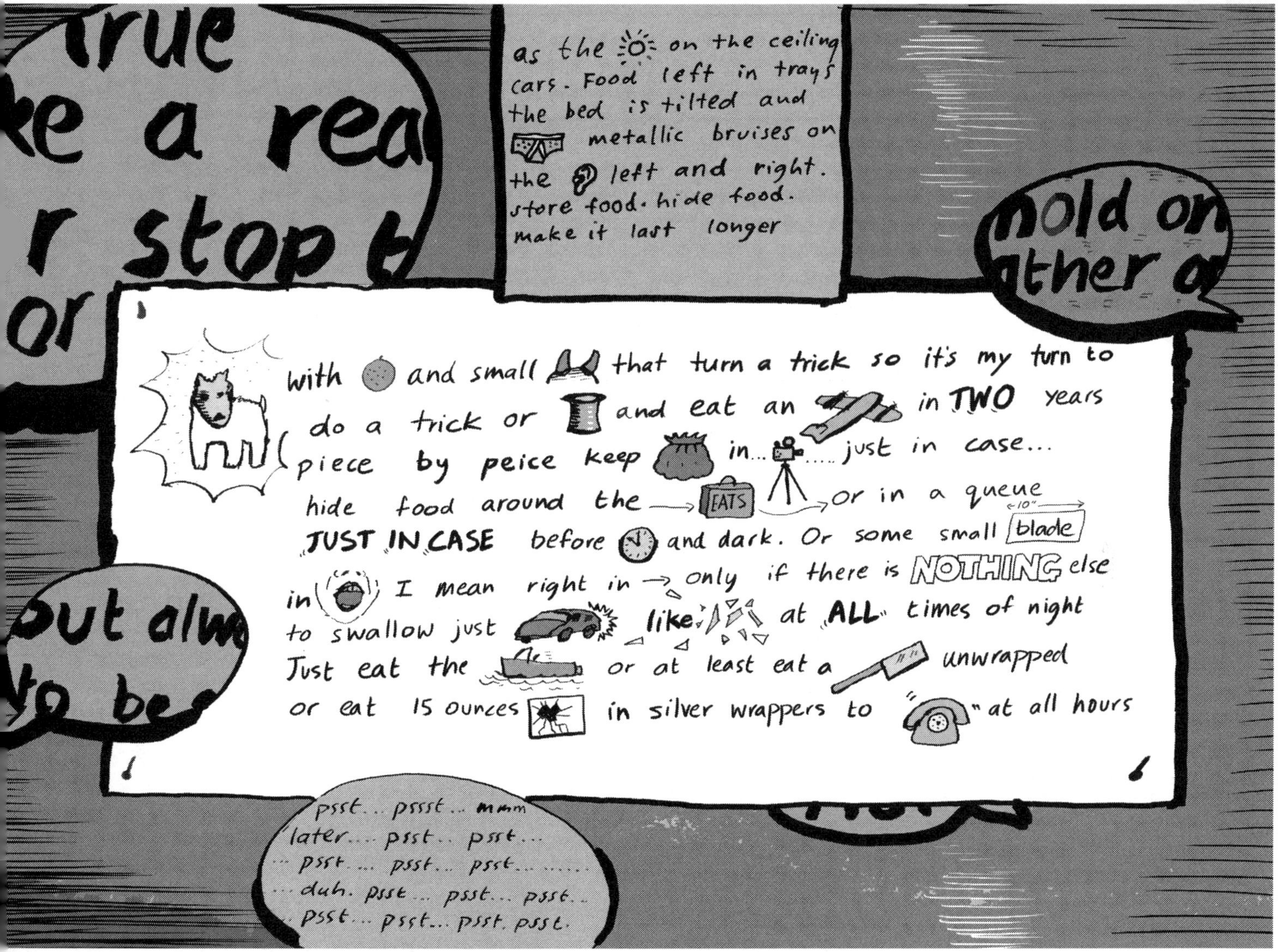

true
ke a rea
r stop
or
as the on the ceiling cars. Food left in trays the bed is tilted and metallic bruises on the left and right. store food. hide food. make it last longer
hold on
ther a
with and small that turn a trick so it's my turn to
do a trick or and eat an in TWO years
piece by peice keep in... ..... just in case...
hide food around the EATS or in a queue 10"
JUST IN CASE before and dark. Or some small blade
in I mean right in only if there is NOTHING else
to swallow just like at ALL times of night
Just eat the or at least eat a unwrapped
or eat 15 ounces in silver wrappers to at all hours
ut alw
o be
psst... pssst... mmm
later.... psst.. psst...
... psst ... psst... psst... .....
... duh. psst ... psst... psst..
psst... psst... psst. psst.

wake me up at 11 or at 12 switch on tv make a sandwich make fries clean the carpet sand the wall make ice and coke feed the dog take a pill
makes a deal for a on carpets. ~~Fries~~ at 10 o'clock. Visitors with lavender or and maps of the city. shops open late. Discount furniture stores
all the

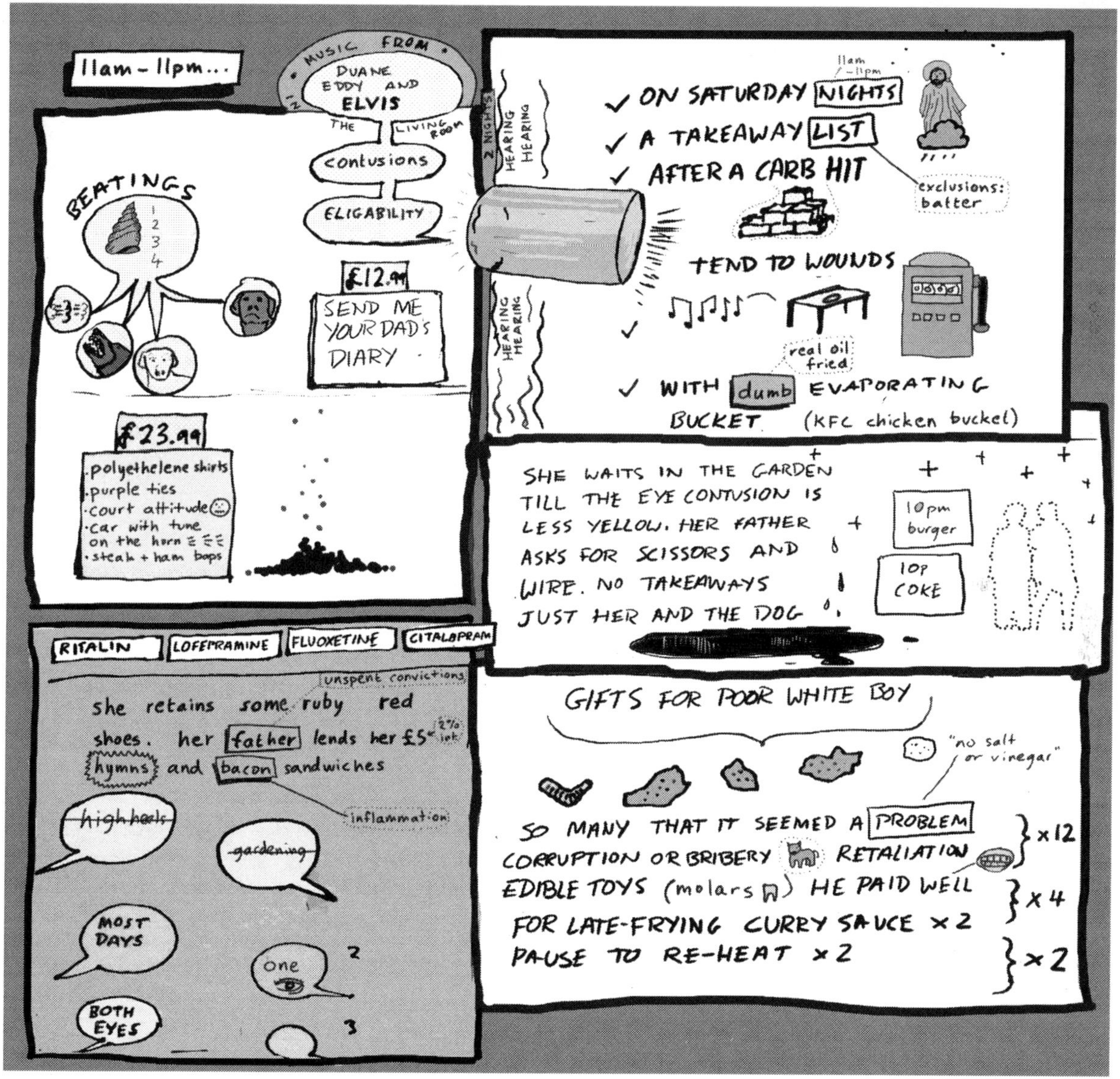
11am – 11pm...
MUSIC FROM
DUANE EDDY AND ELVIS
IN THE LIVING ROOM
contusions
ELIGABILITY
BEATINGS
1
2
3
4
£12.99
SEND ME YOUR DAD'S DIARY
£23.99
.polyethelene shirts
.purple ties
.court attitude
.car with tune on the horn
.steak + ham baps
2 NIGHTS
HEARING HEARING
HEARING HEARING
11am – 11pm
✓ ON SATURDAY NIGHTS
✓ A TAKEAWAY LIST
exclusions: batter
✓ AFTER A CARB HIT
TEND TO WOUNDS
real oil fried
✓ WITH dumb EVAPORATING BUCKET (KFC chicken bucket)
SHE WAITS IN THE GARDEN TILL THE EYE CONTUSION IS LESS YELLOW. HER FATHER ASKS FOR SCISSORS AND WIRE. NO TAKEAWAYS JUST HER AND THE DOG
10pm burger
10p COKE
RITALIN
LOFEPRAMINE
FLUOXETINE
CITALOPRAM
unspent convictions
she retains some ruby red shoes. her father lends her £5 hymns and bacon sandwiches
2% int
inflammation
high heels
gardening
MOST DAYS
one
2
BOTH EYES
3
GIFTS FOR POOR WHITE BOY
"no salt or vinegar"
SO MANY THAT IT SEEMED A PROBLEM
CORRUPTION OR BRIBERY RETALIATION
EDIBLE TOYS (molars) HE PAID WELL
FOR LATE-FRYING CURRY SAUCE × 2
PAUSE TO RE-HEAT × 2
× 12
× 4
× 2

chapter six

LAMENT 1

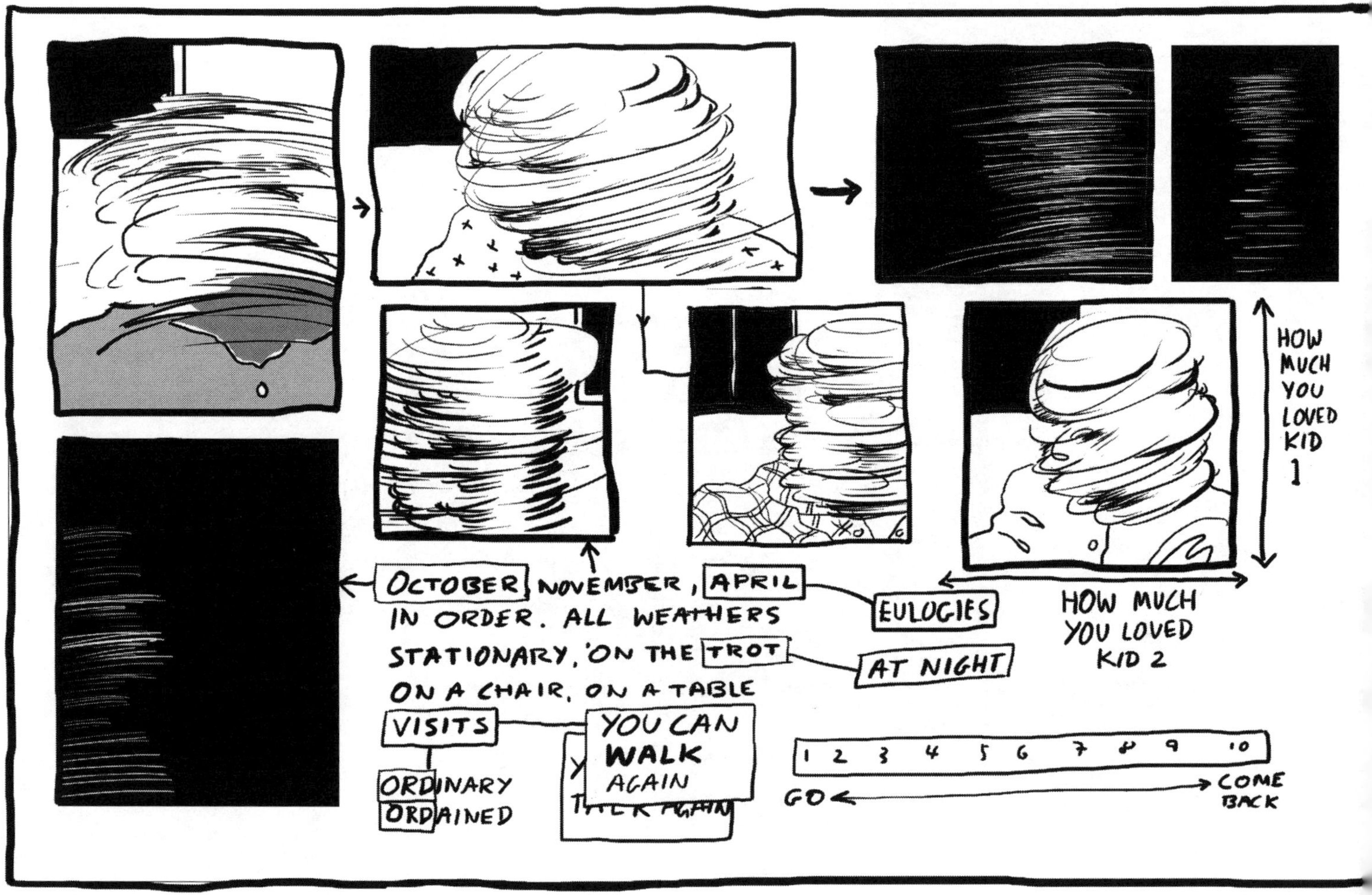
HOW MUCH YOU LOVED KID 1
OCTOBER, NOVEMBER, APRIL
IN ORDER. ALL WEATHERS
STATIONARY, 'ON THE TROT
ON A CHAIR, ON A TABLE
EULOGIES
AT NIGHT
HOW MUCH YOU LOVED KID 2
VISITS
ORDINARY
ORDAINED
YOU CAN WALK AGAIN
Y
TALK AGAIN
1 2 3 4 5 6 7 8 9 10
GO
COME BACK

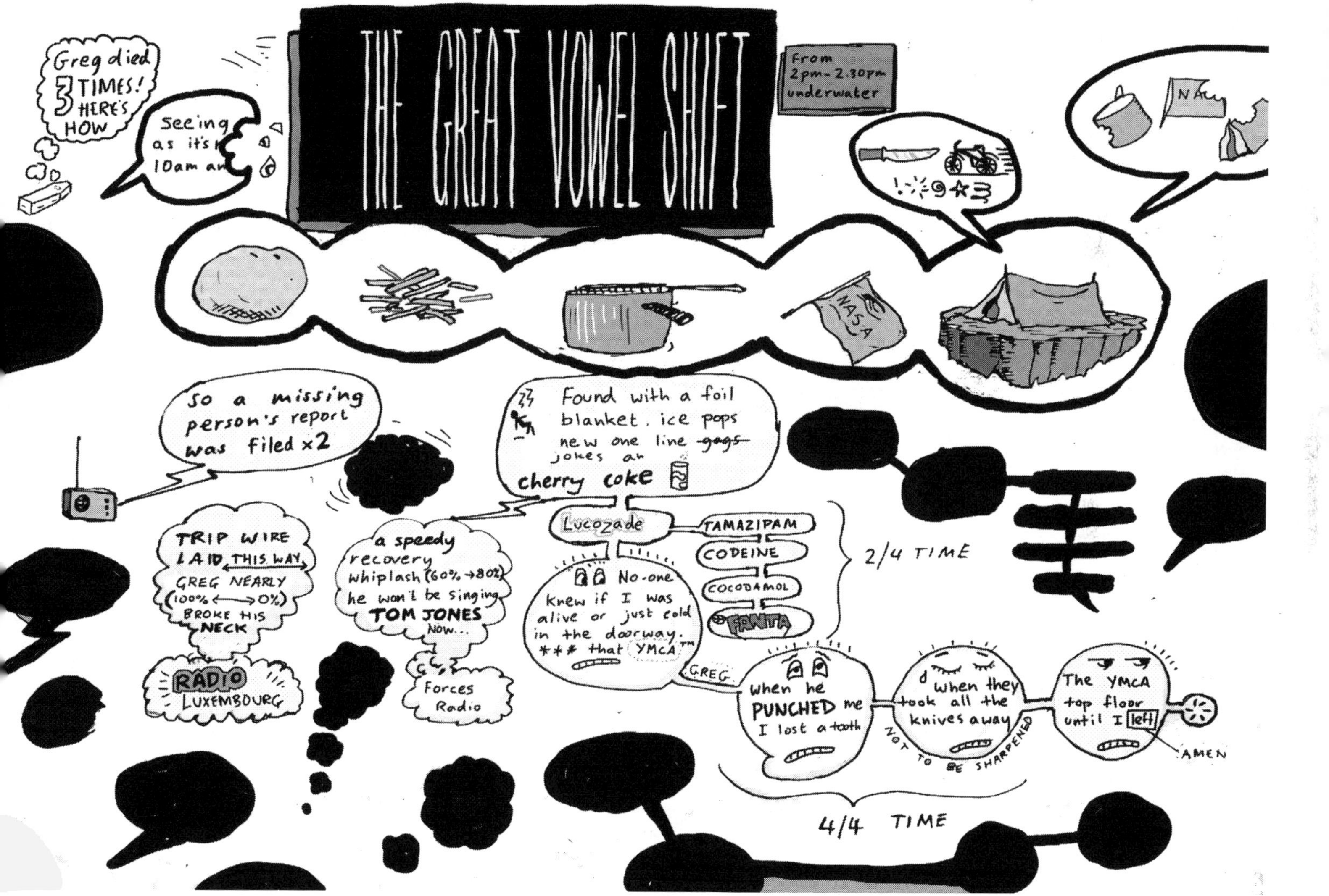
THE GREAT VOWEL SHIFT
Greg died 3 TIMES! HERE'S HOW
Seeing as it's 10am an
From 2pm-2.30pm underwater
NASA
So a missing person's report was filed x2
Found with a foil blanket, ice pops new one line gags jokes an cherry coke
TRIP WIRE LAID THIS WAY GREG NEARLY (100% ⟷ 0%) BROKE HIS NECK
RADIO LUXEMBOURG
a speedy recovery whiplash (60% → 80%) he won't be singing TOM JONES NOW...
Forces Radio
Lucozade
TAMAZIPAM
CODEINE
COCODAMOL
FANTA
2/4 TIME
No-one knew if I was alive or just cold in the doorway. *** that YMCA™
GREG
When he PUNCHED me I lost a tooth
When they took all the knives away
NOT TO BE SHARPENED
The YMCA top floor until I left
AMEN
4/4 TIME

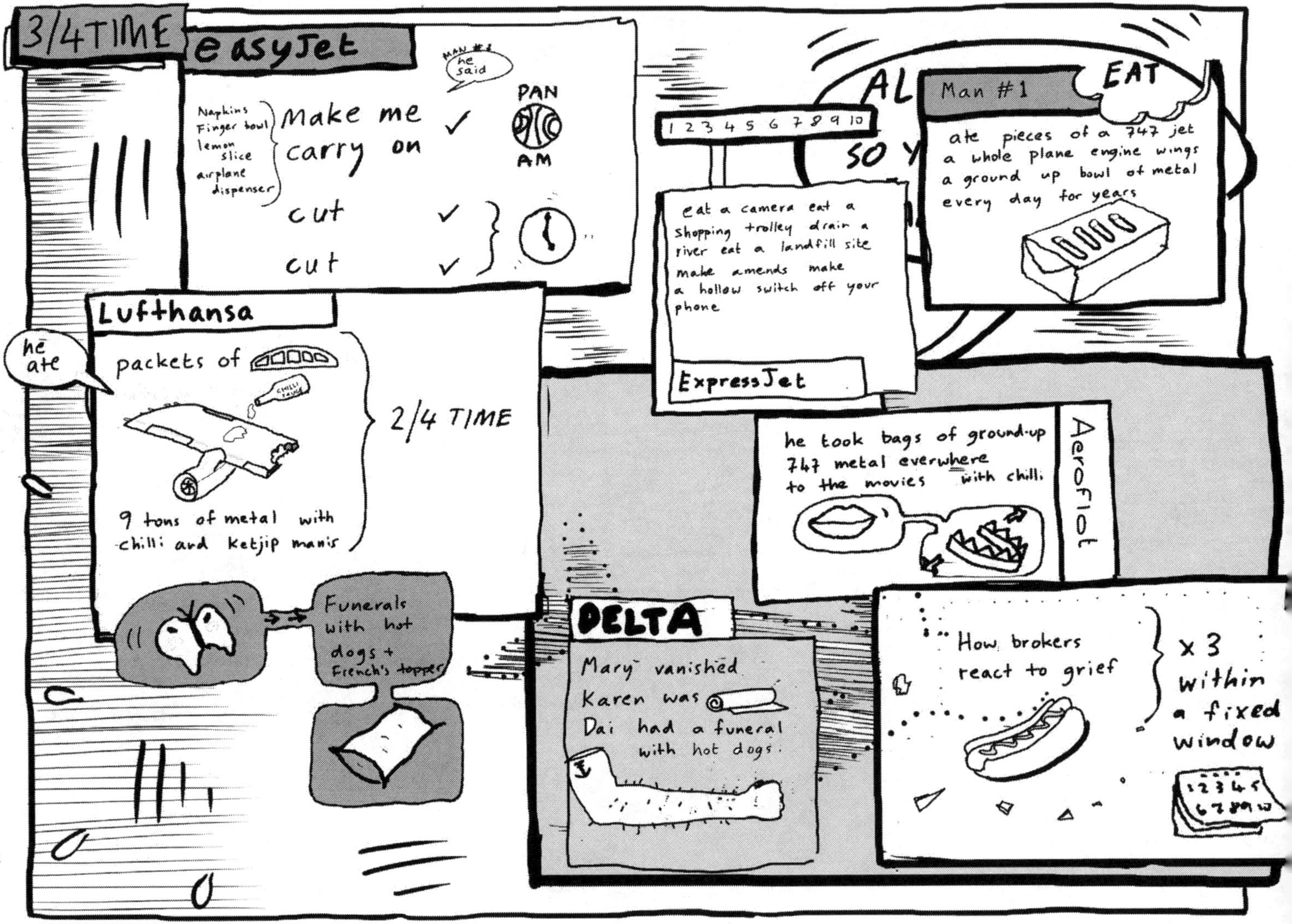

3/4TIME
easyJet
MAN #1 he said
Napkins
Finger bowl
lemon slice
airplane dispenser
Make me carry on ✓
PAN AM
cut ✓
cut ✓
1 2 3 4 5 6 7 8 9 10
eat a camera eat a shopping trolley drain a river eat a landfill site make amends make a hollow switch off your phone
ExpressJet
Man #1
EAT
ate pieces of a 747 jet a whole plane engine wings a ground up bowl of metal every day for years
Lufthansa
he ate
packets of
CHILLI SAUCE
9 tons of metal with chilli and ketjip manis
2/4 TIME
Funerals with hot dogs + French's topper
he took bags of ground-up 747 metal everwhere to the movies with chilli
Aeroflot
DELTA
Mary vanished Karen was Dai had a funeral with hot dogs.
How brokers react to grief
x 3 within a fixed window

TAKEN IN
1
PUNCH
STRIPED
CARDIGUN
PISSED
=2/10
#
AIR PRESSURE
-2°C
SLUMPED
WITH FOIL BLANKET
PULL
S-SSSNAP.
CITALAPRAM
KLICK
KLICK
SHOOT
SCORE
1 2 3 4 5
ZOOOOM
I WISH I HAD MORE TIME
TO SPEND FINDING A YMCA THAT WILL ACCOMMODATE YOUR HEROIN HABIT
MOUNTAINS OF TIME
ALL THE LOVE IN THE WORLD
NO NEED TO PLAN FOR A PENSION
AND GET TO KNOW HOW YOU LIKE YOUR FISH FINGERS
2OZ FOR $20
MR PIGGY
1 2 3
CASH RETURN DEPOSITS
PING
PING
FUNERAL COSTS
THE YMCA KICKED YOU OUT
COILED TIGHT
ALRIGHT WEMBLEY
ZING
YMCA - NADA -NADA-
BUT...
HE WAS HOLY ON WEED
CHILLI
DEATH DUTIES
BANK OF TEETH
1 2 3
20,000
20,000
HEATING
EATING
11.30 am
HE TRIED TO FLIRT WITH THE PALL BEARER
11.37am

TAKE ME HOME - SEASON 1
AGE 18...
ATTITUDE YOU NEED
SUNDAY THRU MONDAY
LITTLE SHITTY ATTITUDE... BUSTER
MOTHER OF GOD ATTITUDE
HAIR GEL
SMOKES, SMOKES UNTIL.....
AGE 21
HOT AIR
AGE 41
COOL AIR ATTITUDE
RESURRECTION ATTITUDE
12 DISC SET OF TAKE ME HOME
0 — 1 — 2 — 3 — JUMP 5 — 6 — 7 — JUMP 8 - 9 — 10 — JUMP

TWO VISITS BY DEAD BROTHERS
pst. psst
psst
pst.
pst
pst
pst
psk. ps
hmm
Monday
Tuesd
Thursday
Friday
hmm... psst... psst
[redacted]
storage solutions
strokes of a canoe
spins a knot in the air
the oil rubs on your
glut of air like rock
you inhale like a cable tube
and carpet rails
is pressed on your jaw on visit number
a perfect impression of your jaw
clothes
resin
cross-irons
amber rock
two
BLACK MOULD ON THE WA
TICK-TICK
TICK-TICK
TIC
TICK-TICK
TICK
TICK
SPORES next to your head
so you kicked the wall and that did it
those blots and if or when
we both breathed like that in bleach
in then the other
TICKETS
1
2
3
4
scratchcards 1, 3, 20,
numbers 9, 12, [redacted], 41, [redacted]

MOST HAUNTED
+
csi: miami
+
csi: new york
+
E R
+
unsolved mysteries
+
Lost without a trace
scooby-do
+
murder by the sea
+
pay for breakages
+
home alone
+
urban legends

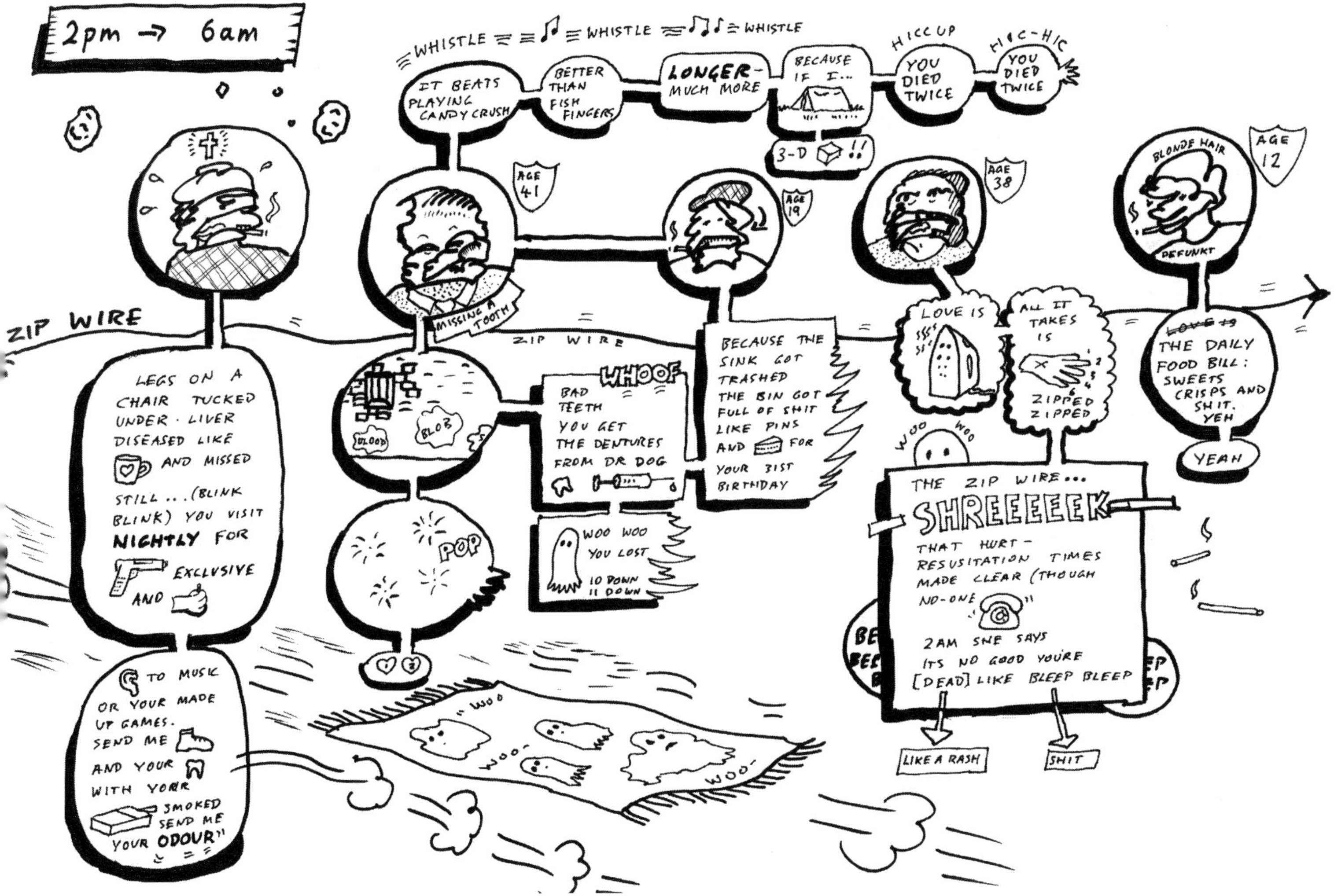
2pm → 6am
WHISTLE
WHISTLE
WHISTLE
IT BEATS PLAYING CANDY CRUSH
BETTER THAN FISH FINGERS
LONGER- MUCH MORE
BECAUSE IF I...
3-D !!
HICCUP
YOU DIED TWICE
HIC-HIC
YOU DIED TWICE
AGE 41
AGE 19
AGE 38
BLONDE HAIR
AGE 12
DEFUNKT
MISSING A TOOTH
ZIP WIRE
ZIP WIRE
LEGS ON A CHAIR TUCKED UNDER · LIVER DISEASED LIKE AND MISSED STILL ... (BLINK BLINK) YOU VISIT NIGHTLY FOR EXCLUSIVE AND
TO MUSIC OR YOUR MADE UP GAMES. SEND ME AND YOUR WITH YOUR SMOKED SEND ME YOUR ODOUR"
BLOOD
BLOB
POP
WHOOF
BAD TEETH YOU GET THE DENTURES FROM DR DOG
WOO WOO YOU LOST 10 DOWN 11 DOWN
BECAUSE THE SINK GOT TRASHED THE BIN GOT FULL OF SHIT LIKE PINS AND FOR YOUR 31ST BIRTHDAY
LOVE IS
ALL IT TAKES IS ZIPPED ZIPPED
LOVE IS THE DAILY FOOD BILL: SWEETS CRISPS AND SHIT. YEH
YEAH
WOO WOO
THE ZIP WIRE...
SHREEEEEK
THAT HURT- RESUSITATION TIMES MADE CLEAR (THOUGH NO-ONE "
2AM SHE SAYS ITS NO GOOD YOU'RE [DEAD] LIKE BLEEP BLEEP
LIKE A RASH
SHIT
WOO
WOO-
WOO-

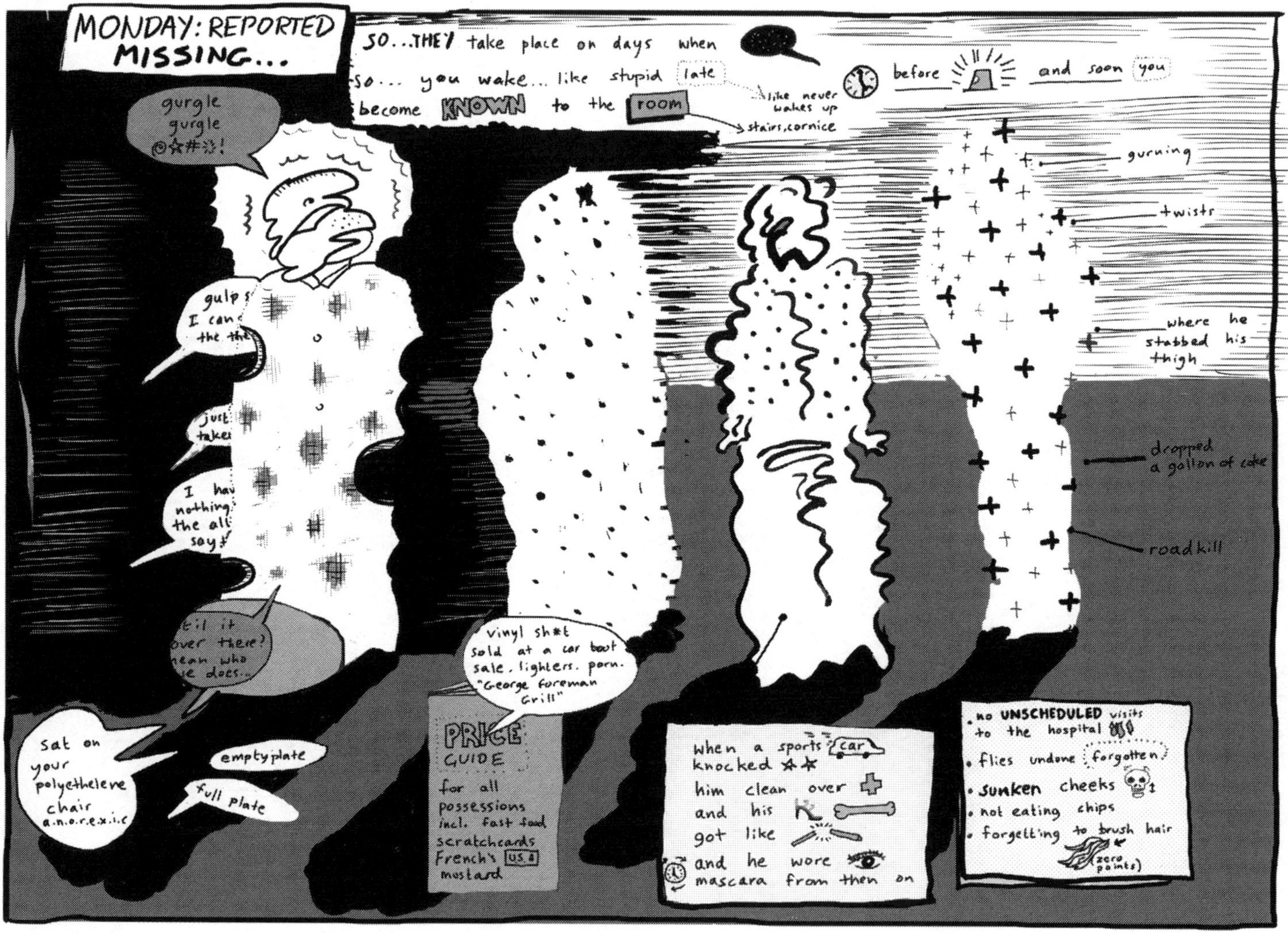
MONDAY: REPORTED MISSING...
SO...THEY take place on days when
so... you wake... like stupid late
like never wakes up
before
and soon you
become KNOWN to the room
stairs, cornice
gurgle gurgle @☆#☼!
gurning
twists
where he stabbed his thigh
dropped a gallon of coke
roadkill
vinyl sh*t sold at a car boot sale, lighters, porn. "George Foreman Grill"
Sat on your polyethelene chair a.n.o.r.e.x.i.c
empty plate
full plate
PRICE GUIDE
for all possessions incl. fast food scratchcards French's U.S.A mustard
when a sports car knocked ☆☆ him clean over and his got like and he wore mascara from then on
no UNSCHEDULED visits to the hospital
flies undone forgotten
sunken cheeks
not eating chips
forgetting to brush hair
(zero points)

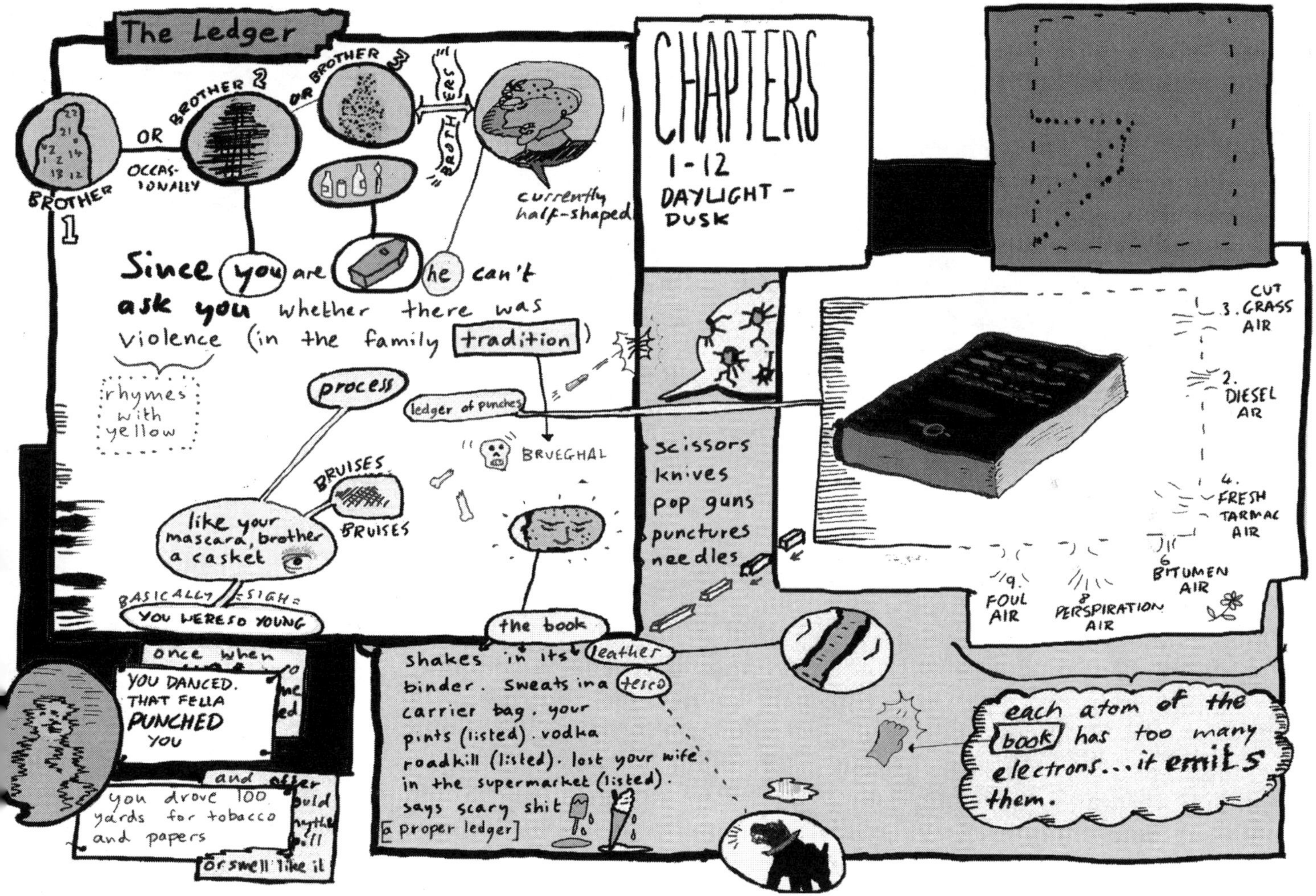

The Ledger
BROTHER 1
OR
BROTHER 2
OCCAS-IONALLY
OR BROTHER 3
"BROTHERS"
currently half-shaped
Since you are he can't ask you whether there was violence (in the family tradition)
rhymes with yellow
process
ledger of punches
BRUEGHAL
BRUISES
BRUISES
BRUISES
like your mascara, brother a casket
BASICALLY = SIGH =
YOU WERESO YOUNG
the book
CHAPTERS
1-12
DAYLIGHT - DUSK
scissors
knives
pop guns
punctures
needles
CUT 3. GRASS AIR
2. DIESEL AIR
4. FRESH TARMAC AIR
6 BITUMEN AIR
8 PERSPIRATION AIR
9. FOUL AIR
once when
YOU DANCED. THAT FELLA PUNCHED YOU
and after
you drove 100 yards for tobacco and papers
or smell like it
shakes in its leather binder. sweats in a tesco carrier bag. your pints (listed). vodka roadkill (listed). lost your wife in the supermarket (listed). says scary shit
[a proper ledger]
each atom of the book has too many electrons... it emits them.

MIDWINTER...
KSSSSSSS
KSHHHHHH
KSHSSSSS
SHHHKRRRRAK
WAP-WAP
BAM
YOUR EYES TAKE A BATTERING
C# F.SHARP
NOTHING BEATS TV LATE
SHADES OF BLACK
TUESDAY ⟷ FRIDAY
WASTE FOOD
MUD + WATER
SPLATT
SCRAPED ELBOWS KNEE OUT OF JOINT
SCARY MAN
↳ MALLORY
↳ JONESY
↳ MICKEY
↳ STICKSY
HICK-OMETER
DUCK, SWING COMMIT GBH
X YEARS
TRY NEW PILLS VS PULL HAIR + TEETH
FINISH BY 3PM THE NEXT SHIFT STARTS

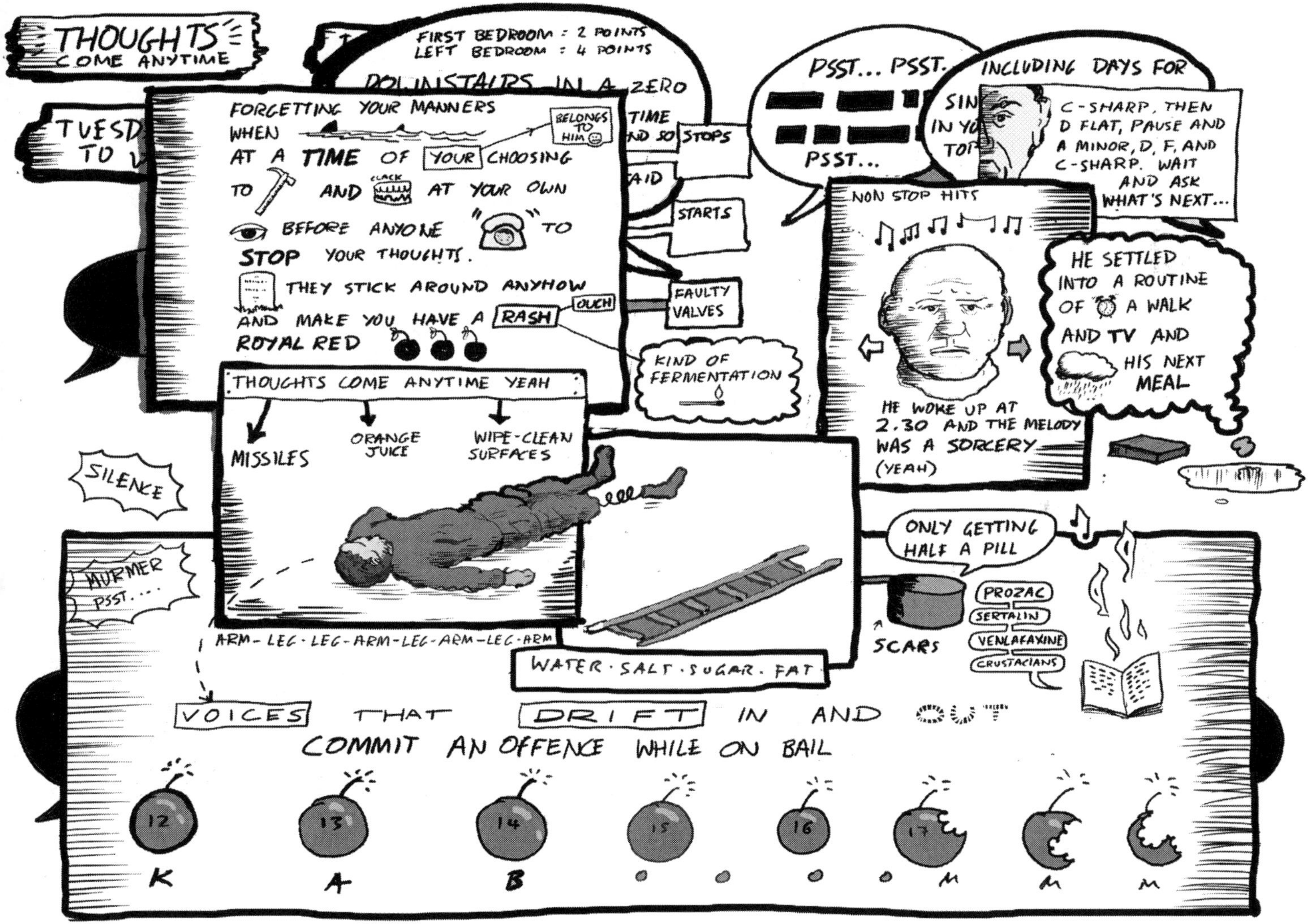

THOUGHTS COME ANYTIME
FIRST BEDROOM : 2 POINTS
LEFT BEDROOM : 4 POINTS
FORGETTING YOUR MANNERS WHEN
BELONGS TO HIM
AT A TIME OF YOUR CHOOSING
TO AND CLACK AT YOUR OWN
BEFORE ANYONE TO
STOP YOUR THOUGHTS.
THEY STICK AROUND ANYHOW
AND MAKE YOU HAVE A RASH
OUCH
ROYAL RED
STOPS
STARTS
FAULTY VALVES
KIND OF FERMENTATION
PSST... PSST...
[redacted]
PSST...
INCLUDING DAYS FOR
C-SHARP, THEN D FLAT, PAUSE AND A MINOR, D, F, AND C-SHARP. WAIT AND ASK WHAT'S NEXT...
NON STOP HITS
HE WOKE UP AT 2.30 AND THE MELODY WAS A SORCERY (YEAH)
HE SETTLED INTO A ROUTINE OF A WALK AND TV AND HIS NEXT MEAL
THOUGHTS COME ANYTIME YEAH
MISSILES
ORANGE JUICE
WIPE-CLEAN SURFACES
SILENCE
MURMER PSST....
ARM-LEG-LEG-ARM-LEG-ARM-LEG-ARM
WATER · SALT · SUGAR · FAT
ONLY GETTING HALF A PILL
PROZAC
SERTALIN
VENLAFAXINE
CRUSTACIANS
SCARS
VOICES THAT DRIFT IN AND OUT
COMMIT AN OFFENCE WHILE ON BAIL
12
13
14
15
16
17
K
A
B
M
M
M

KOSHHH
FZZZZ
KER-WHUMP
KSSHH
CLICK-A-CLICK
-A-CLICK-CLICK
WUMP
KRRRANNNG
TAP-TAP-TAP
TAP-TAP-
TAP

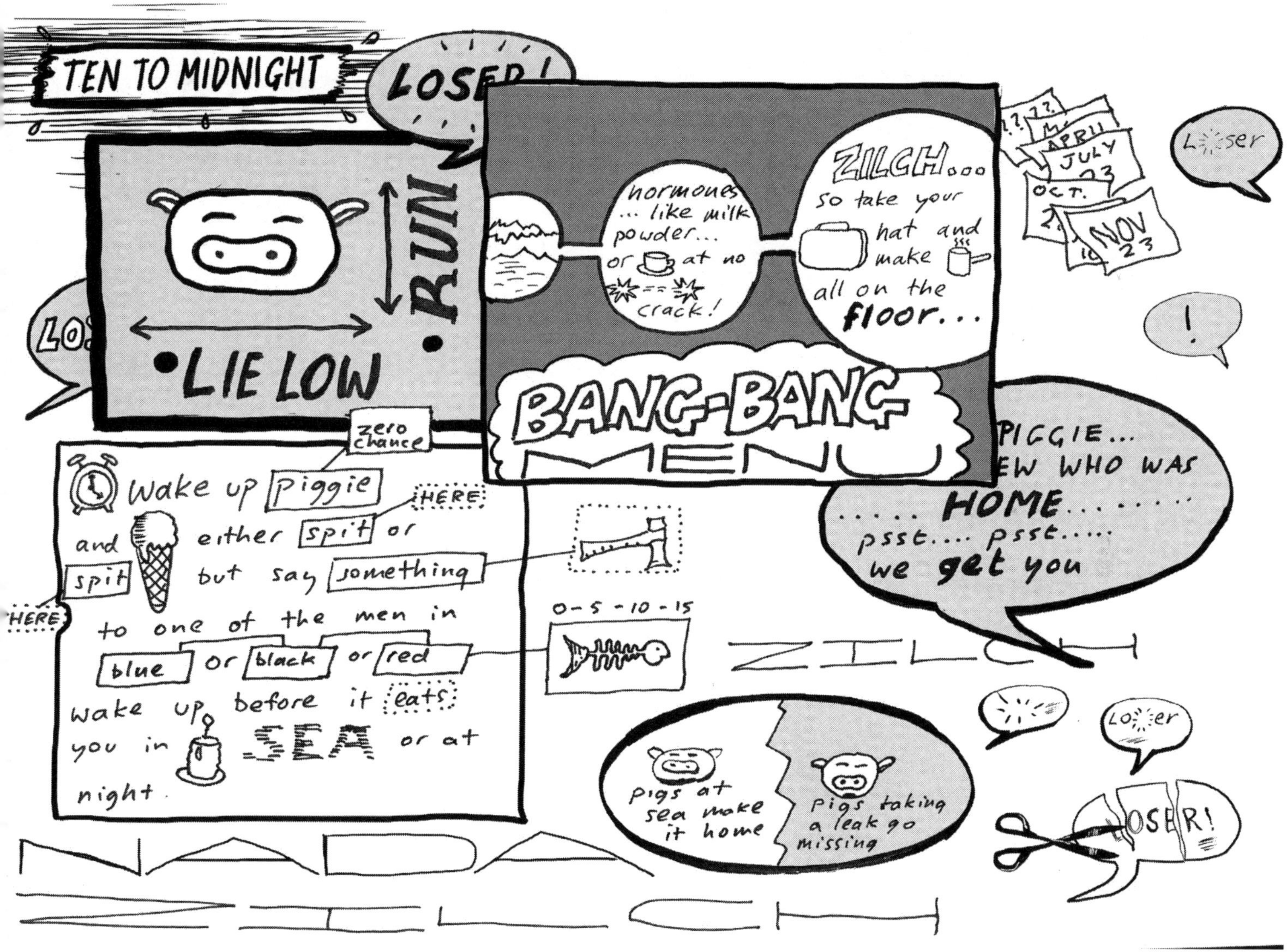
TEN TO MIDNIGHT
LOSER!
RUN
LIE LOW
hormones ... like milk powder... or at no crack!
ZILCH... so take your hat and make all on the floor...
BANG-BANG MENU
zero chance
Wake up piggie and either spit or spit but say something to one of the men in blue or black or red wake up before it eats you in SEA or at night.
HERE
HERE
0-5-10-15
PIGGIE... EW WHO WAS HOME ..... psst.... psst.... we get you
ZILCH
JULY
OCT.
NOV 23
APRIL
!
pigs at sea make it home
Pigs taking a leak go missing
LOSER!
NADA
ZILCH

THE B/SHOP ~~KNOW~~ KNEW YOU
[LIKED] ✓
YOU ALWAYS READ - 24/7
BELLOW, ROTH, YEAH
YOU GAVE UP SMOKING
EVERYONE LOVED YOU
YOU WOULD BE BA-HAI OR AT LEAST KIND TO ANIMALS
YOU BURNT THE FISH FINGERS—EVERY TIME
PSST...PSST

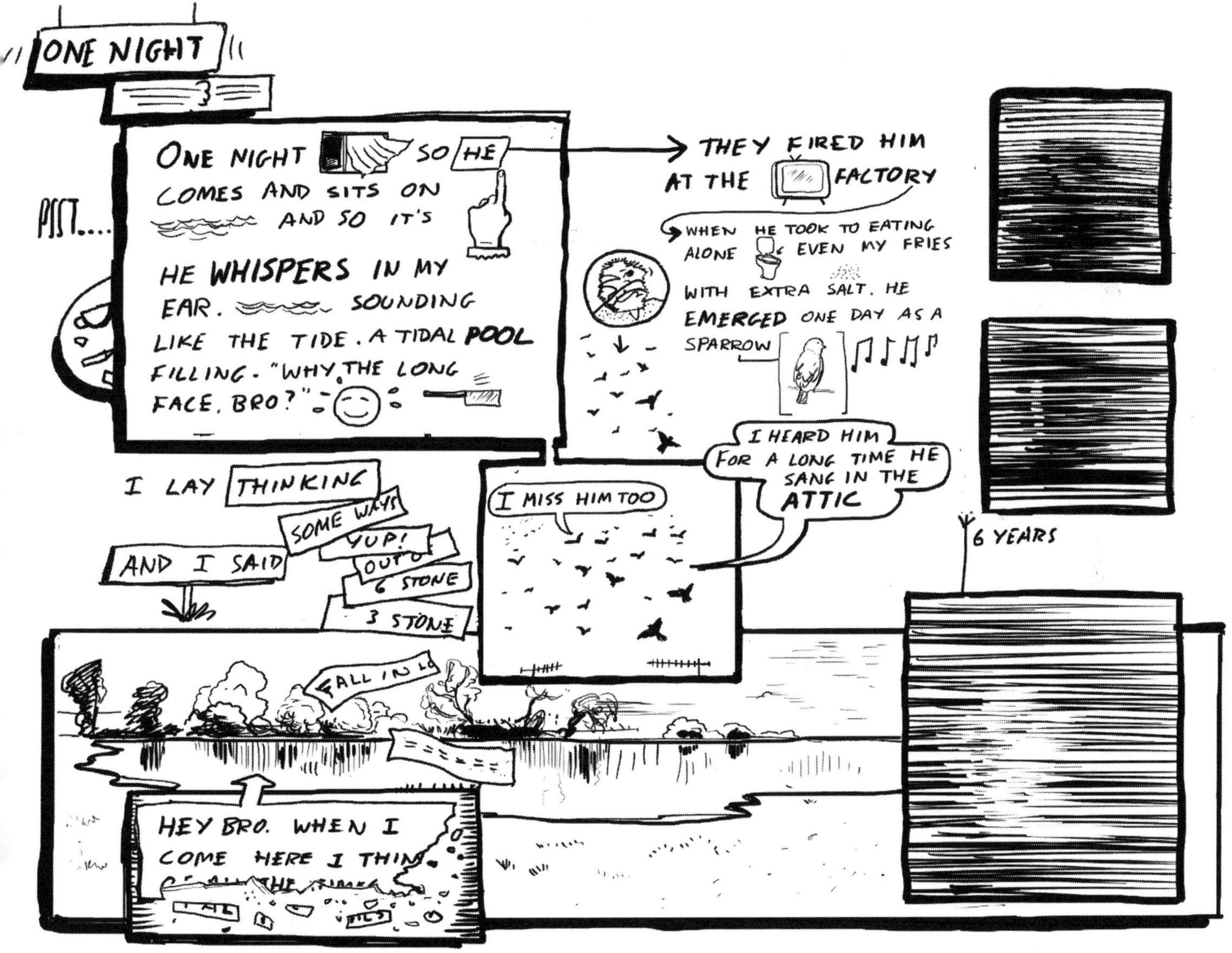
ONE NIGHT
PSST....
ONE NIGHT SO HE COMES AND SITS ON AND SO IT'S
HE WHISPERS IN MY EAR. SOUNDING LIKE THE TIDE. A TIDAL POOL FILLING. "WHY THE LONG FACE, BRO?"
THEY FIRED HIM AT THE FACTORY
WHEN HE TOOK TO EATING ALONE EVEN MY FRIES WITH EXTRA SALT. HE EMERGED ONE DAY AS A SPARROW
I LAY THINKING
AND I SAID
SOME WAYS
YUP!
6 STONE
3 STONE
I MISS HIM TOO
I HEARD HIM FOR A LONG TIME HE SANG IN THE ATTIC
6 YEARS
FALL IN LO
HEY BRO. WHEN I COME HERE I THIN

AUTHOR BIO

Russell Evans is a Welsh artist and writer. His visual poems have been published in *Iterant, 3am Magazine, Heavy Feather* and others. He holds a PhD in visual poetry and teaches at a university in England.

Evans wrote two books on filmmaking and exhibits in galleries in New York, Italy and the UK.

www.russellevans.net

ACKNOWLEDGMENTS

This collection would not be possible without the inspiration of Deborah Maier and Golda Solomon and the writers at Blue Door Arts Center, New York.

I also owe so much to Wendy for encouragement and reminding me what it's all for.

Gratitude to Bianca Stone for her ideas and insights.

And a huge thank you to tara caribou, a relentless supporter of writers, and everyone at Raw Earth Ink.

Made in the USA
Monee, IL
07 November 2026

68085974R00044